Fresh Ways with Fish and Shellfish

COVER
Baked sole takes on a whole new guise when it is wrapped round prawns and asparagus and dressed with a purée of tomatoes, shallots and prawn stock. Fresh dill provides additional flavour and colour (recipe, page 40).

TIME-LIFE BOOKS
EUROPEAN EDITOR: Ellen Phillips
Design Director: Ed Skyner
Director of Editorial Resources: Samantha Hill
Chief Sub-Editor: Ilse Gray

Correspondents: Elisabeth Kraemer-Singh (Bonn); Dorothy Bacon (London); Maria Vincenza Aloisi, Josephine du Brusle (Paris); Ann Natanson (Rome)

HOW THINGS WORK
SYSTEM EARTH
LIBRARY OF CURIOUS AND UNUSUAL FACTS
BUILDING BLOCKS
A CHILD'S FIRST LIBRARY OF LEARNING
VOYAGE THROUGH THE UNIVERSE
THE THIRD REICH
MYSTERIES OF THE UNKNOWN
TIME-LIFE HISTORY OF THE WORLD
FITNESS, HEALTH & NUTRITION
HEALTHY HOME COOKING
UNDERSTANDING COMPUTERS
THE ENCHANTED WORLD
LIBRARY OF NATIONS
PLANET EARTH
THE GOOD COOK
THE WORLD'S WILD PLACES

Sixth European English language printing 1992.

ISBN 0 7054 2004 3
TIME-LIFE is a trademark of Time Warner Inc. U.S.A.

HEALTHY HOME COOKING
SERIES DIRECTOR: Dale M. Brown
Deputy Editor: Barbara Fleming
Series Administrator: Elise Ritter Gibson
Designer: Herbert H. Quarmby
Picture Editor: Sally Collins
Photographer: Renée Comet
Text Editor: Allan Fallow
Editorial Assistant: Rebecca C. Christoffersen

Editorial Staff for *Fresh Ways with Fish and Shellfish*
Book Manager: Susan Stuck
Assistant Picture Editor: Scarlet Cheng
Writer: Margery A. duMond
Researcher/Writer: Andrea E. Reynolds
Copy Co-ordinators: Marfé Ferguson Elizabeth Graham, Norma Karlin
Picture Co-ordinator: Linda Yates
Photographer's Assistant: Rina M. Ganassa

European Edition:
Designer: Lynne Brown
Sub-Editor: Wendy Gibbons
Production Co-ordinator: Maureen Kelly
Production Assistant: Deborah Fulham

THE COOKS

ADAM DE VITO began his cooking apprenticeship when he was only 14. He has worked at Le Pavillon restaurant in Washington D.C., taught with cookery author Madeleine Kamman, and conducted classes at L'Académie de Cuisine in Maryland.

HENRY GROSSI was awarded a Grand Diplôme at the École de Cuisine La Varenne in Paris. He then served as the school's assistant director and as its North American business and publications co-ordinator.

JOHN T. SHAFFER is a graduate of The Culinary Institute of America at Hyde Park, New York. He has had a broad experience as a chef, including five years at the Four Seasons Hotel in Washington, D.C.

CONSULTANTS

CAROL CUTLER is the author of many cookery books. During the 12 years she lived in France, she studied at the Cordon Bleu and the École des Trois Gourmandes, as well as with private chefs. She is a member of the Cercle des Gourmettes and a charter member and past president of Les Dames d'Escoffier.

NORMA MACMILLAN has written several cookery books and edited many others. She has worked on various cookery publications, including *Grand Diplôme* and *Supercook*. She lives and works in London.

PAT ALBUREY is a home economist with a wide experience of preparing foods for photography, teaching cookery and creating recipes. She has been involved in a number of cookery books and was the studio consultant for the Time-Life series *The Good Cook*.

JOYCE NETTLETON, who has a doctorate from the Harvard School of Public Health, is the author of *Seafood Nutrition*, a source book for the seafood industry and health and nutrition professionals. A registered dietician, she has produced several award-winning nutrition education booklets and promoted good nutrition on radio and television.

NUTRITION CONSULTANTS

JANET TENNEY has been involved in nutrition and consumer affairs since she received her master's degree in human nutrition from Columbia University. She is the manager for developing and implementing nutritional programmes for a major chain of supermarkets.

PATRICIA JUDD trained as a dietician and worked in hospital practice before returning to university to obtain her MSc and PhD degrees. Since then she has lectured in Nutrition and Dietetics at London University.

Nutritional analyses for *Fresh Ways with Fish and Shellfish* were derived from Practicaire's Nutriplanner System and other current data.

This volume is one of a series of illustrated cookery books that emphasizes the preparation of healthy dishes for today's weight-conscious, nutrition-minded eaters.

HEALTHY HOME COOKING

Fresh Ways with Fish and Shellfish

BY

THE EDITORS OF TIME-LIFE BOOKS

TIME-LIFE BOOKS/AMSTERDAM

Contents

Curried Grouper

Baked Grey Mullet

Baked Powan with Garlic and Glazed Carrots

Clams and Rice Yucatan-Style

Warm Mussel and Potato Salad

4 *Microwaving Fish and Shellfish* 113

Red Mullet Marinated in Passion Fruit Juice

Lemon Sole Paupiettes with Ginger and Dill

Techniques 128

A Most Excellent Food

The thought is as welcome as a breath of sea air on a hot summer's day: fish and shellfish contain more native goodness, weight for weight, than almost any other type of food. From the briny tang of a freshly shucked oyster to the majestic savour of a whole poached salmon, they are as healthy as they are delicious. Fish provide one of the most concentrated sources of high-quality protein, with an average 125 g (4 oz) serving yielding up to half the daily dietary requirement of this nutrient. They deliver an uncommonly rich supply of vitamins and minerals as well, and they are easily digested.

At the same time, most varieties recommend themselves to weight-conscious diners. A 125 g (4 oz) portion of haddock or cod, for example, has fewer than 100 calories. Even their fattier cousins, such as salmon and mackerel, have fewer than half the calories of a T-bone steak. Moreover, nearly all fish and shellfish — and this comes as very good news indeed — are low in cholesterol. Even the folk wisdom that holds fish to be "brain food" may have some basis in fact: recent studies have suggested that the fatty acids present in fish may be involved in the development of neural tissue.

More than 100 species of edible fish and shellfish thrive in European waters. There is something to please every palate and accommodate every purse. Plaice and sole have long been relished at the table, as have cod and halibut. But other, less well known fish are available too, and they offer exciting culinary opportunities, as the recipes in this book demonstrate. Much depends on the skill of the cook, to be sure, but it so happens that fish and shellfish are among the simplest of foods to prepare. Cooking times tend to be brief, and such basic methods as steaming, baking and grilling serve best to preserve nutrients and bring out flavours.

Some surprising discoveries

It has long been known that fish and shellfish bestow a generous nutritional dividend, but until quite recently no one knew just how significant the health payoff could be. The leaner varieties of fish have been prized for their modest amounts of calories and cholesterol, but the fattier types — with more than 5 per cent of the edible portion of their bodies consisting of oil — have been cause for concern.

Now the picture has changed. Scientists turning their attention to the eating habits of Greenland Eskimos made a surprising discovery. During the first part of the 20th century, the Eskimos consumed, as they always had, great quantities of fatty fish and marine animals, yet they were astonishingly healthy. Despite their rich diet, heart disease was virtually unknown among them. A more recent study, in the Netherlands, corroborated this: a group of 852 middle-aged Dutch men, who had been eating modest but regular amounts of seafood over a 20-year period, had less than half the likelihood of contracting fatal heart disease than did their non-fisheating compatriots — even though the fish eaters consumed slightly more cholesterol. Then, across the world in Japan, still another study showed that inhabitants of fishing villages, for whom fish was a staple, were virtually free of heart disease.

Fish and marine animals, the scientists determined, contain certain polyunsaturated fats found in no other foods, and these substances were demonstrated to have a profound effect on body chemistry. Fish oil appears to lower the levels of harmful triglycerides (or blood fats) in the blood. Moreover, it behaves quite differently from polyunsaturated vegetable oils in staving off heart disease. The oils from such rich-fleshed swimmers as salmon and mackerel actually discourage the formation of blood clots that can block ailing arteries. Nor is that all. Current studies suggest that fish oil may be beneficial in discouraging breast cancer and such inflammatory diseases as asthma and arthritis. The message comes through loud and clear: fatty fish need not be avoided; their fat has virtues. And, as if this were not enough to make seafood lovers smile, scientists have made some important discoveries about shellfish as well.

Improved analytical techniques have revealed not only that most shellfish are low in cholesterol but that some, notably the shelled molluscs, contain sterols picked up from their vegetarian diet that actually appear to reduce the amount of cholesterol absorbed by the body. Only squid, octopus, prawns and certain varieties of clam and crab have more than 100 milligrams of cholesterol per 100 g (3½ oz) portion; people on low-cholesterol diets should be wary of them, along with fish roe, which is also high in cholesterol.

Further enhancing the reputation of fish and shellfish for being healthy food are their stores of vitamins and minerals. The B vitamins, which the body needs to make proper use of protein and other nutrients, are particularly abundant in tuna, sardines, herring and various shellfish. Healthy blood requires iron and copper, and most shellfish provide both; finned fish with dark meat, such as mackerel, are also good iron sources. A generous dose of phosphorus, essential for strong bones, comes with every fish course. All saltwater varieties provide iodine, and most types provide potassium, fluoride, manganese and magnesium as well. Oysters are exceptionally high in zinc, which helps fight infection, promotes healthy skin, and is used to build more than 100 vital body enzymes.

Pursuing freshness

It goes without saying that fish tastes best when it has just been caught. The sweet quayside taste of a plaice or bass, plucked straight from the ocean and delivered on the plate with a minimum of preparatory fuss, is hard to equal. And for true fish lovers nothing will do but that they go down to the water, fishing rod in hand, and haul in their own dinner. Even then they must take special care to maintain prime freshness. After shellfish, fish is the most perishable of foods. It has a high moisture content, offering bacteria an attractive environment in which to grow. In addition, oils present — particularly in the fattier types — begin to oxidize when they are exposed to air.

Knowledgeable anglers make it a practice to kill and gut each fish as soon as it is taken from the hook. A prompt execution — either by a smart blow on the head or else a quick slap against a hard object to break the backbone — is preferable to a lingering death in the fishnet or on shore or bank. To gut the fish, make a cut from the anal fin towards the head and draw out the viscera *(pages 128-129)*; bacteria lodged in the digestive organs are the first cause of decomposition. Stow the cleaned fish with ferns or seaweed in a creel or other container — or, better still, in an insulated box filled with crushed ice. Back in the kitchen, the fish can be scaled or skinned, or cut into fillets *(pages 128-131)*. If not cooked immediately, it can be rinsed, patted dry, covered and stored for a day or two in the coolest part of the refrigerator.

Many people also like to gather their own shellfish, raking up clams from the shore, setting a crab line or lobster pot, or prising a feast of mussels from rocks or pilings. Provided that the source is an unpolluted body of water, untainted by human or industrial waste, the rewards at the table cannot be excelled. Check with the local authorities that the area is safe. Whatever is collected can be preserved for a day or two in the refrigerator in open containers covered with a damp cloth, but do not keep it any longer.

What to look for

Most of us do our fishing at the fishmongers, but a few simple guidelines will help to bring home the freshest catch available. The first priority is to find a reliable supplier — and the signs of a really good one are very evident. Every surface will be scrupulously clean, and a sweet, briny fragrance will fill the air. The fish will be laid out on ice in bins, or set in pans and kept just short of freezing. Most selections will have their heads kept on, and their skins will display a maritime rainbow of shimmering colour. A good fishmonger will cut only as many fillets and steaks as he knows he can sell that day, since fish keeps best when left intact. There may be a tank of live lobsters in sea water, or a bin of iced crabs still twitching their claws. Turnover will be rapid, and what is on display today will usually be gone by tomorrow.

In making a choice for the dinner table, let your decision be guided by what is freshest. Clams and oysters should clamp up tightly when touched. Mussels, on the other hand, may keep their shells partly open, but these should stay rigidly in position. Lobsters and crabs should be lively. Squid should have firm, creamy-coloured skin. When it comes to finned fish, good sense suggests a variety that is locally in season; it will tend to be both cheaper and fresher. But the nationwide distribution of commercial fish has become so efficient, with daily shipments sent out from processing centres by refrigerated lorry or aeroplane, that a wide selection is usually available. Aquaculture has increased the year-round availability of certain species such as rainbow trout and salmon. These farm-grown specimens are scientifically fed, then harvested when they reach a certain size and sent immediately to market.

Fresh fish is sold whole, or cut into steaks, cutlets or fillets. Your fishmonger will dress a whole fish for you — remove the head fins and tail, scale it and gut it — or you can do this yourself. Buying a whole fish has advantages; it will have been handled less and will have lost fewer of its juices. Photographs on pages 130 and 131 show how you can slice your own fillets from whole fish.

When a whole fish is truly fresh, its eyes are clear, bright and slightly protruding, with shiny black pupils. The gills are pinkish or bright red; brown gills signal a stale specimen. The skin will be firm and bright. The scales will adhere to it tightly. The flesh of most fish will feel firm and elastic to the touch. And a fresh fish smells fresh, with a subtle clean fragrance suggestive to some of cucumber, to others of the sea itself. A fishy odour is a sure sign of

The Key to Better Eating

Healthy Home Cooking addresses the concerns of today's weight-conscious, health-minded cooks with recipes that take into account guidelines set by nutritionists. The secret of eating well, of course, has to do with maintaining a balance of foods in the diet. The recipes thus should be used thoughtfully, in the context of a day's eating. To make the choice easier, this book presents an analysis of nutrients in a single serving of each fish or shellfish recipe, as on the right. The counts for calories, protein, cholesterol, total fat, saturated fat and sodium are approximate. Among other things, the fat content of fish can vary, depending on the season, where the fish was caught, and the species. For fish cooked with the skin on, data are not yet available for the skin's calories and fat.

Calories **180**
Protein **21g**
Cholesterol **65mg**
Total fat **8g**
Saturated fat **4g**
Sodium **230mg**

Interpreting the chart

The chart below gives dietary guidelines for healthy men, women and children. Recommended figures vary from country to country, but the principles are the same everywhere. Here, the average daily amounts of calories and protein are from a report by the U.K. Department of Health and Social Security; the maximum advisable daily intake of fat is based on guidelines given by the National Advisory Committee on Nutrition Education (NACNE); those for cholesterol and sodium are based on upper limits suggested by the World Health Organization.

The volumes in the Healthy Home Cooking series do not purport to be diet books, nor do they focus on health foods. Rather, they express a commonsense approach to cooking that uses salt, sugar, cream, butter and oil in moderation while employing other ingredients that also provide flavour and satisfaction. Herbs, spices and aromatic vegetables, as well as fruits, peels, juices, wines and vinegars are all employed towards this end.

The recipes make few unusual demands. Naturally they call for fresh ingredients, offering substitutes when these are unavailable. (The substitute is not calculated in the nutrient analysis, however.) Most of the ingredients can be found in any well-stocked supermarket.

In order to simplify meal planning, most of the recipes offer accompaniments. These accompaniments are intended only as suggestions, however; cooks should let their imaginations be their guide and come up with ideas of their own to achieve a sensible and appealing balance of foods.

In Healthy Home Cooking's test kitchens, heavy-bottomed pots and pans are used to guard against burning the food whenever a small amount of oil is used and where there is danger of the food adhering to the hot surface, but non-stick pans can be utilized as well. Both safflower oil and virgin olive oil are favoured for sautéing. Safflower oil was chosen because it is the most highly polyunsaturated vegetable fat available in supermarkets, and polyunsaturated fats reduce blood cholesterol; if unobtainable, use sunflower oil, also high in polyunsaturated fats. Virgin olive oil is used because it has a fine fruity flavour lacking in the lesser grade known as "pure". In addition, it is — like all olive oil — high in monounsaturated fats, which are thought not to increase blood cholesterol. When virgin olive oil is unavailable, or when its flavour is not essential to the success of the dish, "pure" may be used.

About cooking times

To help the cook plan ahead, Healthy Home Cooking takes time into account in its recipes. While recognizing that everyone cooks at a different speed, and that stoves and ovens differ, the series provides approximate "working" and "total" times for every dish. Working time stands for the minutes actively spent on preparation; total time includes unattended cooking time, as well as time devoted to marinating, steeping or soaking ingredients. Since the recipes emphasize fresh foods, they may take a bit longer to prepare than "quick and easy" dishes that call for canned or packaged products, but the payoff in flavour, and often in nutrition, should compensate for the little extra time involved.

Recommended Dietary Guidelines

		Average Daily Intake		**Maximum Daily Intake**			
		CALORIES	PROTEIN *grams*	CHOLESTEROL *milligrams*	TOTAL FAT *grams*	SATURATED FAT *grams*	SODIUM *milligrams*
Females	7-8	1900	47	300	80	32	2000*
	9-11	2050	51	300	77	35	2000
	12-17	2150	53	300	81	36	2000
	18-54	2150	54	300	81	36	2000
	54-74	1900	47	300	72	32	2000
Males	7-8	1980	49	300	80	33	2000
	9-11	2280	57	300	77	38	2000
	12-14	2640	66	300	99	44	2000
	15-17	2880	72	300	108	48	2000
	18-34	2900	72	300	109	48	2000
	35-64	2750	69	300	104	35	2000
	65-74	2400	60	300	91	40	2000

* *(or 5g salt)*

deterioration. Members of the shark and skate families give off a slight ammonia scent, but this is natural and will disappear.

The task of identifying truly fresh fish is more difficult when it comes to steaks or fillets. But here, too, appearances count. Each piece should be firm and its cut surfaces should be moist, not dried out, with no sliminess and no browning or yellowing at the edges. Nor should there be any smell of fishiness. If the fish is prepackaged, there should be little air space between the fish and wrapping, and little or no liquid in the package (pass up any fish in milky-coloured fluid).

When fresh fish fails to meet these criteria, a frozen specimen may be the preferred option. Indeed, most supermarket fish is sold this way. But bear in mind that any intermediate thawing and refreezing between the processing centre and the supermarket (or between the home freezer and table, for that matter) take an unfortunate toll. Buy only frozen packages that are solid, without interior air pockets. Reject any that have torn wrappings or exterior coatings of frost. Discoloration of the fish is a telltale sign of freezer burn, which occurs when moisture is lost through faulty packaging and which destroys flavour.

The amount of seafood to buy, whether frozen or fresh, depends on how it will be cooked, and of course on how much is to be eaten. A standard portion of fish or shellfish would be about 125 to 175 g (4 to 6 oz) of cooked meat, not counting bones or shells (this book emphasizes a 125 g/4 oz serving). Thus, if a fish is to be purchased whole, you should allow as much as 350 g (12 oz) for each diner; but if it is already dressed, about 250 g (8 oz) per person will be ample. Half a dozen clams or oysters make the customary half-shell first course. When buying fresh prawns, remember that about half their weight consists of heads and shells.

Ensuring flavour and nutrition

Once home from the shop, seafood tastes best when it is promptly used. If fish cannot be cooked on the day of its purchase, it should be rinsed in cold water, dried with paper towels, swathed tightly in plastic film and stored for not more than two days in the coolest part of the refrigerator.

Longer intervals of storage require that the fish be frozen. Whether it is purchased at the shop or proudly borne home from a morning's fishing expedition, the method is the same. The gutted fish should be scaled, if necessary; it can then be cut into fillets, steaks or chunks, or kept whole, as desired. After rinsing the fish under cold running water, pat it dry with paper towels and wrap it in aluminium foil or moistureproof polythene, with as much air excluded as possible; air is the arch villain of freezer burn. The packets should be spaced loosely in the freezer to promote rapid chilling. If freezer temperatures are held down to a frigid 18°C (0°F), fatty fish can be stored for up to three months, and leaner varieties for six months. But for the best flavour, all frozen fish should be served within one or two months. Do not attempt to freeze shellfish; some, like prawns, may have already been frozen because of their perishability. Refreezing them will serve only to rob them of more flavour and texture.

In thawing fish, proceed slowly. Thaw each packet in the refrigerator, well in advance of the time the fish is to be cooked; allow 24 hours for each 500 g (1 lb). Do not thaw fish at room temperature; bacteria will quickly start to grow. Once the fish is thawed, wash it again gently and dry it once more to get rid of any bacteria that might be present on the surface.

No matter how carefully a potential seafood dinner has been selected or stored, its moment of truth comes in the kitchen. The role of the cook is much like that of a classical pianist: to render fully each nuance of texture and flavour, with verve and freshness, but without undue violence or distortion. The recipes in this book are designed to do just that. They rely on basic, easily mastered cooking methods that work most effectively in transmitting both nutrients and taste. Only deep frying is omitted, for obvious health reasons. (Nor is the eating of raw freshwater fish recommended, because of the possibility of parasites.) The first section takes up the lean varieties of finned fish, along with the cooking methods that suit them best. Their fattier relatives are discussed in the second section. Shellfish are the focus of the third section, and the final section introduces the special procedures for cooking fish and shellfish in a microwave oven. A glossary, beginning on page 137, defines and describes fish and shellfish called for by the recipes in the book.

Since they are naturally tender, fish and shellfish benefit from short cooking times. The recipes give specific heats, and most recommend that you test the fish for doneness after the indicated time. A general guideline for all cooking methods is to give the fish 10 minutes for every 2.5 cm (1 inch) of flesh measured at its thickest point. (When baking, set the oven at 230°C, 450°F, or Mark 8.) Not only is it essential that fish and shellfish be cooked carefully, but also that they be served right away.

In the recipes that follow, sauces are kept light and delicate — designed to enhance, not mask, the seafood's innate goodness. They often incorporate the fish's juices or depend on fish stock for subtlety of flavour (a recipe for fish stock appears on page 136). An inventive scheme of seasonings and sauce bases replaces the calorie-charged elaborations of tradition. Delivered to the table with its virtues intact, each dish seems to carry with it the roar of the surf or the gurgle of the trout stream.

1 *Fresh from the sea, lean fish — bass, flounder and red snapper among others — shimmer on a bed of shaved ice.*

Beneficent, Lean-Fleshed Fish

More low-fat fish come to market year round than any other kind — and no wonder. They are among the most popular of commonly eaten saltwater and freshwater specimens. All of them are rich in protein and miserly in calories, with a fat content of no more than 5 per cent and frequently of less than 2 per cent. The fat they do possess is found mainly in the liver, which is removed in cleaning.

Lean fish tend to be mild in flavour, with tender, flaky white or pale flesh that lends itself to varied culinary treatments. But because lean fish tend to dry out during cooking, techniques that preserve or add moisture — notably sautéing or steaming — are ideal. Most varieties may also be cooked successfully in the oven, provided they are supplied with additional moisture, smothered in a blanket of vegetables, or wrapped in parchment paper or foil so that they can steam in their own juices. Some may even be grilled or barbecued, if they are generously basted.

Among the leanest of the lean are such flat fish as plaice and sole, with their pancake-like bodies and delicate, fine-textured flesh. One of the nicest things about flat fish is that they may be substituted for one another in a dish. What is more, they are relatively easy to prepare; photographs on page 131 show how to fillet and skin them.

Techniques for cleaning and filleting lean round fish — so described because their bodies are tubular in shape — are demonstrated on pages 128-130. In this section, such ever-popular round fish as cod and haddock get fresh treatment. Cod made into fishcakes acquires new character when served with a horseradish sauce, and haddock is transformed when baked in enchiladas topped with a chili sauce.

Enterprising cooks who would like to try less familiar fish will find interesting recipes for several varieties. One of these calls for mahimahi — or dolphin fish — a brightly-scaled denizen of subtropical waters; the fish is stuffed with a spicy filling, baked and then topped with sliced, toasted almonds. Skate is poached, and the poaching liquid becomes the base for a vinaigrette-like sauce containing slices of crunchy green beans and sweet red pepper. Shark, long shunned at dining tables but now receiving deserved attention from adventurous cooks, is stir-fried with Chinese cabbage in a mild dish that belies this predator's nasty reputation. One bite into a piece of shark so prepared will prove that eating it amounts to sweet revenge indeed.

Sea Bass with 20 Cloves of Garlic

Serves 4
Working time: about 20 minutes
Total time: about 1 hour

Calories **200**
Protein **23g**
Cholesterol **45mg**
Total fat **10g**
Saturated fat **1g**
Sodium **210mg**

600 g	*sea bass steaks (or halibut)*	*1¼ lb*
2 tbsp	*safflower oil*	*2 tbsp*
2	*sweet red peppers, diced*	*2*
20	*garlic cloves, very thinly sliced*	*20*
1	*fresh hot green chili pepper, seeded and finely chopped (caution, page 45)*	*1*
6 tbsp	*finely chopped fresh coriander, plus several whole sprigs for garnish*	*6 tbsp*
¼ tsp	*salt*	*¼ tsp*
	freshly ground black pepper	
1 tsp	*paprika, preferably Hungarian*	*1 tsp*
½ litre	*fish stock (recipe, page 136) or dry white wine*	*16 fl oz*

Rinse the fish under cold running water and pat it dry with paper towels. Remove any scales from the skin; if the steaks are large, cut them in half lengthwise.

Heat the oil over medium heat in a heavy frying pan large enough to hold the fish in one layer. Add the red pepper and sauté it lightly for 2 minutes. Add the garlic, green chili and chopped coriander; reduce the heat to low and cook, stirring frequently, for 1 minute. Place the fish on top of the vegetables and sprinkle it with the salt, some pepper and the paprika. Pour in the stock or wine and bring the liquid to a simmer, basting the fish occasionally. Cover, and reduce the heat to low. Cook until the fish is opaque — about 8 minutes.

With a slotted spoon, transfer the fish to a deep platter. Remove the skin from the steaks. Cover the platter with aluminium foil to keep the fish from drying out while you finish the sauce.

Boil the liquid in the pan, stirring occasionally, until only about 12.5 cl (4 fl oz) remain — 5 to 10 minutes. Pour the sauce over the fish. Serve at room temperature or cold, garnished with the coriander sprigs.

SUGGESTED ACCOMPANIMENTS: *green salad; bread rolls.*

Pike with Onions, Cabbage and Apple

Serves 6
Working time: about 25 minutes
Total time: about 1 hour

Calories **200**
Protein **18g**
Cholesterol **50mg**
Total fat **6g**
Saturated fat **2g**
Sodium **145mg**

1.5 kg	*whole pike (or carp)*	*3 lb*
1 tbsp	*safflower oil*	*1 tbsp*
3	*onions, thinly sliced*	*3*
250 g	*cabbage, thinly sliced*	*8 oz*
¼ litre	*dry white wine*	*8 fl oz*
1 tbsp	*cider vinegar*	*1 tbsp*
¼ tsp	*caraway seeds*	*¼ tsp*
¼ tsp	*salt*	*¼ tsp*
	freshly ground black pepper	
1	*red apple, cored and cut into wedges*	*1*
25 g	*unsalted butter*	*¾ oz*
1 tbsp	*finely cut chives*	*1 tbsp*

To loosen the scales of the pike, scald the fish: put it in the sink or a large basin and pour a kettle of boiling water over it. Scale and clean the fish *(pages 128-129)*. Cut off and discard the head.

Preheat the oven to 230°C (450°F or Mark 8). Heat the oil in a large, heavy frying pan over medium-high heat. Add the onions and sauté them until they are translucent — about 4 minutes. Add the cabbage, white wine, cider vinegar, caraway seeds, salt and some pepper, and stir well. Bring the liquid to the boil, then reduce the heat to medium and simmer the mixture for 10 minutes.

Transfer the vegetable mixture to a baking dish large enough to accommodate the pike. Set the pike on top of the vegetables and arrange the apple wedges around it. Bake the fish until the flesh is opaque and feels firm to the touch — about 20 minutes.

Transfer the pike and the apples to a heated serving platter and cover them with aluminium foil; set the platter aside while you finish cooking the cabbage and onions. Return the cabbage-and-onion mixture to the frying pan and cook it over high heat until only about 4 tablespoons of liquid remain — approximately 10 minutes. Add the butter and stir until it melts. Place the vegetables round the fish on the serving platter, sprinkle the chives over the fish and serve immediately.

SUGGESTED ACCOMPANIMENTS: *rice pilaff; broad beans.*

Marinated Pike with Cabbage Salad

Serves 4
Working time: about 30 minutes
Total time: about 2 hours and 45 minutes

Calories **400**
Protein **45g**
Cholesterol **125mg**
Total fat **12g**
Saturated fat **4g**
Sodium **370mg**

1.5 kg	*pike*	*3 lb*
	Marinade	
3 tbsp	*clear honey*	*3 tbsp*
2 tbsp	*low-sodium soy sauce or shoyu*	*2 tbsp*
1 tsp	*whole grain mustard*	*1 tsp*
¼ tsp	*cayenne pepper*	*¼ tsp*
1 tbsp	*tomato paste*	*1 tbsp*
1 tsp	*finely grated fresh ginger root*	*1 tsp*
1	*garlic clove, crushed*	*1*
4 tbsp	*dry white wine*	*4 tbsp*
1	*orange, rind only, finely grated*	*1*
3 tbsp	*orange juice*	*3 tbsp*
	Cabbage salad	
350 g	*white cabbage*	*12 oz*
1 tbsp	*virgin olive oil*	*1 tbsp*
1	*lemon, rind only, finely grated*	*1*
1 tbsp	*lemon juice*	*1 tbsp*
½ tsp	*caraway seeds*	*½ tsp*
½ tsp	*salt*	*½ tsp*
	freshly ground black pepper	

Carefully fillet the pike, as demonstrated on page 130. Remove the skin from the fillets. Cut the fillets into neat 2.5 cm (1 inch) cubes, removing any small bones that you find.

Put all the ingredients for the marinade into a large bowl and mix them together. Add the pike cubes to the marinade, stir well until the cubes are evenly coated, then cover and leave the fish to marinate for 2 to 3 hours.

Thirty minutes before cooking the pike, make the salad. Cut the cabbage into very fine shreds. In a bowl, mix together the olive oil, lemon rind and juice, caraway seeds, salt and pepper. Add the cabbage to this dressing and mix well. Spoon the dressed salad into a shallow serving dish, cover the dish and set it aside until ready to serve.

Preheat the grill. Remove the pike cubes from the marinade and thread the pieces on to wooden skewers. Cook under a hot grill for 4 to 5 minutes until the pike is cooked, turning the skewers half way through cooking. Do not overcook the pike because it will dry out. Arrange the skewers on top of the salad and serve at once.

SUGGESTED ACCOMPANIMENT: *tomato salad.*

Lemon Sole on a Bed of Mushrooms and Spinach

Serves 4
Working (and total) time: about 35 minutes

Calories **210**
Protein **27g**
Cholesterol **75mg**
Total fat **10g**
Saturated fat **1g**
Sodium **305mg**

500 g	*lemon sole fillets, skinned*	*1 lb*
350 g	*mushrooms, wiped clean and sliced*	*12 oz*
1	*lemon, juice only*	*1*
	freshly ground black pepper	
500 g	*fresh spinach, washed and stemmed, or 300 g (10 oz) frozen spinach, thawed*	*1 lb*
2 tbsp	*safflower oil*	*2 tbsp*
1	*onion, finely chopped*	*1*
⅛ tsp	*grated nutmeg*	*⅛ tsp*
¼ tsp	*salt*	*¼ tsp*

Put the mushrooms in a saucepan with the lemon juice and a generous grinding of pepper. Pour in enough water to cover them, then bring the liquid to the boil. Reduce the heat to medium and simmer the mixture until the mushrooms are tender — about 5 minutes. Set the pan aside.

Put the fresh spinach, with water still clinging to its leaves, in a large pan over medium heat. Cover the pan and steam the spinach until the leaves are wilted — 2 to 3 minutes. (Frozen spinach needs no cooking.) Squeeze the moisture from the spinach and chop it coarsely.

Heat 1 tablespoon of the oil in a large, heavy frying pan over medium heat. Add the onion and cook it until it is translucent — about 4 minutes. Drain the mushrooms and add them to the pan, then stir in the spinach and cook for 2 minutes. Season the mixture with the nutmeg, salt and some pepper, then spread it evenly in the bottom of a fireproof baking dish.

Preheat the grill. Rinse the fillets under cold running water and pat them dry with paper towels. Fold the fillets into three and lay them on the vegetable mixture. Brush with the remaining oil and grill until the flesh flakes easily when tested with a fork — about 5 minutes. Serve immediately.

SUGGESTED ACCOMPANIMENT: *boiled new potatoes.*

Sole Fillets with Wine and Grape Sauce

Serves 4 as a starter
Working (and total) time: about 40 minutes

Calories **250**
Protein **23g**
Cholesterol **130mg**
Total fat **10g**
Saturated fat **4g**
Sodium **155mg**

2	*Dover soles (about 750 g/1½ lb each)*	*2*
30 cl	*fish stock (recipe, page 136)*	*½ pint*
15 cl	*dry white wine*	*¼ pint*
15 g	*unsalted butter, softened*	*½ oz*
15 g	*flour*	*½ oz*
175 g	*green grapes, halved, seeds removed*	*6 oz*
2 tbsp	*double or single cream*	*2 tbsp*
	Garnish	
60 to 90 g	*black grapes*	*2 to 3 oz*

Skin and fillet the soles as illustrated on pages 129 and 131. With the skinned side on the inside, fold each fillet neatly into three.

Place the fillets in a shallow saucepan in a single layer, then pour in the fish stock. Cover the saucepan and simmer the fillets for 5 to 6 minutes, until they are just cooked.

With a slotted spoon, carefully lift the fillets from the saucepan on to paper towels to drain, then arrange them on a warm serving dish. Cover and keep warm while making the sauce.

Boil the fish stock rapidly until it is reduced to 15 cl (¼ pint), then add the white wine. In a small bowl, blend the butter and flour together to make a smooth paste. Using a whisk, incorporate the butter into the stock a little at a time. Continue to stir the sauce with the whisk until it comes to the boil. Reduce the heat to low, add the green grapes and simmer the sauce for 3 to 4 minutes.

Stir the cream into the sauce and heat through for 1 minute, without boiling. Spoon the sauce over the poached sole fillets, garnish with the black grapes and serve immediately.

SUGGESTED ACCOMPANIMENTS: *mange-tout; steamed rice.*

Dover Sole with Orange and Herbs

Serves 2
Working time: about 20 minutes
Total time: about 50 minutes

Calories **170**
Protein **25g**
Cholesterol **100mg**
Total fat **5g**
Saturated fat **2g**
Sodium **320mg**

1	*Dover sole (750 g to 1 kg/1½ to 2 lb), cleaned*	*1*
1	*large orange, peeled, all pith removed, cut into thin slices*	*1*
15 g	*unsalted butter, melted*	*½ oz*
1 tbsp	*mixed chopped fresh herbs (parsley, chives, chervil and dill)*	*1 tbsp*
¼ tsp	*salt*	*¼ tsp*
	freshly ground black pepper	
	sprigs of fresh herbs for garnish	
	grated orange rind	

Preheat the oven to 200°C (400°F or Mark 6).

Remove both black and white skin from the sole, as demonstrated on page 129. Cut off the head and remove any remaining viscera. Using kitchen scissors, cut away the fins from each side of the sole. Rinse the fish under cold water, then pat it dry with paper towels.

Lightly butter a large shallow ovenproof dish and place the sole in the dish. Arrange the orange slices in a neat overlapping row down the centre of the fish.

Pour the melted butter over the sole, then sprinkle the top with the chopped herbs, and season with salt and pepper. Cover the dish with foil and cook the sole in the oven for 25 to 30 minutes, until the flesh flakes easily.

Garnish the sole with herb sprigs and grated orange rind. Serve immediately.

Sea Bass Fillets with Cracked Anise and Mustard Seeds

Calories **190**
Protein **22g**
Cholesterol **60mg**
Total fat **9g**
Saturated fat **4g**
Sodium **230mg**

Serves 4
Working time: about 15 minutes
Total time: about 25 minutes

2	*skinned sea bass fillets (or Norway haddock), about 250 g (8 oz) each, cut in half on the diagonal*	2
1	*shallot, finely chopped*	1
2 tsp	*aniseeds or fennel seeds*	2 tsp
1 tbsp	*mustard seeds*	1 tbsp
30 g	*dry breadcrumbs*	1 oz
2 tsp	*fresh thyme, or ½ tsp dried thyme*	2 tsp
	freshly ground black pepper	
30 g	*unsalted butter*	1 oz
1	*garlic clove, very finely chopped*	1
½	*lemon, juice only*	½
¼ tsp	*salt*	¼ tsp

Preheat the oven to 240°C (475°F or Mark 9). Lightly butter the bottom of a heavy, shallow baking dish. Sprinkle the chopped shallot into the dish.

Crack the aniseeds or fennel seeds and the mustard seeds with a mortar and pestle, or on a cutting board with the flat of a heavy knife. Transfer the seeds to a wide, shallow bowl or pan, and combine them with the breadcrumbs, thyme and some pepper. Put the butter and garlic into a saucepan and melt the butter.

Rinse the fillets under cold running water and pat them dry with paper towels. Rub the fillets with the lemon juice and sprinkle them with the salt and some pepper. Brush a fillet on both sides with some of the garlic butter, then coat it well with the breadcrumb mixture and lay it on the shallot in the baking dish. Repeat these steps with the remaining fillets. Dribble any remaining garlic butter over the top.

Bake the fish until it feels firm to the touch and the coating is golden-brown — 10 to 12 minutes. Serve immediately.

SUGGESTED ACCOMPANIMENTS: *tomato salad; green beans.*

Crisp Baked Bream with Tomato and Mint

Calories **280**
Protein **22g**
Cholesterol **60mg**
Total fat **15g**
Saturated fat **3g**
Sodium **210mg**

Serves 4
Working time: about 25 minutes
Total time: about 40 minutes

4	*sea bream (or perch or trout), about 250 g (8 oz) each, dressed (pages 128-129)*	4
12.5 cl	*skimmed milk*	4 fl oz
1	*egg white, beaten*	1
45 g	*cornmeal*	1½ oz
20 g	*blanched almonds, chopped*	¾ oz
30 g	*fresh mint, chopped*	1 oz
1	*spring onion, trimmed and thinly sliced*	1
	freshly ground black pepper	
1 tbsp	*safflower oil*	1 tbsp
15 g	*unsalted butter*	½ oz
¼ tsp	*salt*	¼ tsp
2	*large ripe tomatoes, skinned, seeded and finely chopped*	2
1 tbsp	*fresh lime or lemon juice*	1 tbsp
1 tbsp	*red wine vinegar*	1 tbsp

Rinse the dressed bream under cold running water and pat them dry. Mix the milk and egg white in a shallow bowl. Soak the fish in this mixture for 15 minutes, turning them twice. Preheat the oven to 180°C (350°F or Mark 4).

While the fish are soaking, combine the cornmeal, almonds, half the mint, the spring onion and a generous grinding of pepper in a shallow dish. At the end of the soaking time, dredge each fish in the cornmeal mixture to coat it evenly.

Heat the oil and butter in a large, shallow fireproof casserole (preferably one with a non-stick surface) over medium heat. Add the fish and cook them on the first side for 4 minutes. Sprinkle the fish with ⅛ teaspoon of the salt and turn them over; sprinkle them with the remaining salt and cook them on the second side for 2 minutes. Put the casserole in the oven for 15 minutes to finish cooking the fish.

While the fish are baking, make the sauce: combine the tomatoes, the remaining mint, the lime or lemon juice, the vinegar and some pepper in a bowl.

When the fish are done, transfer them to a serving platter; pass the sauce separately.

SUGGESTED ACCOMPANIMENT: *corn on the cob.*

Monkfish with Artichoke Ragout

THIS DISH WAS INSPIRED BY "RAÏTO", A PROVENÇAL SAUCE OF TOMATOES, RED WINE, CAPERS AND BLACK OLIVES.

Serves 4
Working time: about 40 minutes
Total time: about 1 hour

Calories **260**
Protein **21g**
Cholesterol **40mg**
Total fat **8g**
Saturated fat **1g**
Sodium **430mg**

500 g	*monkfish fillets*	*1 lb*
4 tbsp	*distilled white vinegar*	*4 tbsp*
4	*globe artichokes*	*4*
1½ tbsp	*virgin olive oil*	*1½ tbsp*
1	*onion, finely chopped*	*1*
4	*garlic cloves, chopped*	*4*
¼ litre	*red wine*	*8 fl oz*
1.25 kg	*ripe tomatoes, skinned, seeded and chopped, or 800 g (28 oz) canned tomatoes, chopped, juice reserved*	*2½ lb*
6	*oil-cured black olives, stoned and halved*	*6*
½ tsp	*capers*	*½ tsp*
1	*bay leaf*	*1*

Pour enough water into a non-reactive saucepan to fill it about 5 cm (2 inches) deep. Add the vinegar.

To prepare the artichoke bottoms, first break or cut the stalk off one of the artichokes. Snap off and discard the outer leaves, starting at the base and continuing until you reach the pale yellow leaves at the core. Cut the top two thirds off the artichoke. Using a paring knife, shave off any dark green leaf bases that remain on the artichoke bottom. Cut the bottom into quarters; trim away any purple leaves and the fuzzy choke. Then cut each quarter into four wedges and drop them into the vinegar water in the saucepan. Repeat these steps with the remaining artichokes.

Simmer the artichoke bottoms over medium heat until they are tender — about 15 minutes. Drain them and set them aside.

Rinse the fillets and pat them dry; slice them into pieces 4 cm (1½ inches) wide. Pour the oil into a large, heavy frying pan over high heat. Add the monkfish pieces and sear them for 1 minute on each side. Transfer the fish to a plate and set it aside.

Reduce the heat to medium high and cook the onion in the frying pan until it is translucent — about 4 minutes. Stir in the garlic and cook for 1 minute longer. Pour in the wine and cook it until almost no liquid remains — about 5 minutes. Stir in the tomatoes (and reserved juice if using canned tomatoes), the olives, capers and bay leaf. Bring the liquid to the boil and cook until reduced by half — about 5 minutes more.

Put the artichoke pieces in the sauce and set the monkfish pieces on top. Reduce the heat to medium, cover the pan, and cook the fish until it is opaque and feels firm to the touch — about 10 minutes. Transfer the fish to a serving dish. Raise the heat to high and cook the sauce for 1 to 2 minutes to thicken it. Transfer the artichokes to the serving dish; pour the sauce over the artichokes and fish, and serve at once.

Salad of Monkfish and Wild Rice

Serves 8
Working time: about 25 minutes
Total time: about 2 hours

Calories **310**
Protein **18g**
Cholesterol **30mg**
Total fat **8g**
Saturated fat **1g**
Sodium **300mg**

500 g	*monkfish fillets*	*1 lb*
¼ litre	*fish stock or court-bouillon (recipes, page 136)*	*8 fl oz*
4 tbsp	*chopped shallots*	*4 tbsp*
2	*garlic cloves, finely chopped*	*2*
1½ tbsp	*chopped fresh sage, or 1½ tsp dried sage*	*1½ tbsp*
½ tsp	*salt*	*½ tsp*
	freshly ground black pepper	
250 g	*wild rice*	*8 oz*
¼ litre	*dry white wine*	*8 fl oz*
1	*lemon, juice only*	*1*
175 g	*shelled young broad beans, thawed if frozen*	*6 oz*
4 tbsp	*thinly sliced sun-dried tomatoes*	*4 tbsp*
250 g	*mange-tout, strings removed, pods cut diagonally in half*	*8 oz*
3 tbsp	*virgin olive oil*	*3 tbsp*

Pour the stock or court-bouillon and 45 cl (¾ pint) of water into a large saucepan. Add 2 tablespoons of the shallots, half of the garlic and half of the sage, ¼ teaspoon of the salt and some pepper; bring the liquid to the boil. Stir in the rice, reduce the heat to low and partially cover the pan. Simmer the rice with the lid slightly ajar until the rice has absorbed the liquid and is tender — 40 to 50 minutes. ▶

While the rice is cooking, prepare the poaching liquid. In a large, non-reactive sauté pan over medium heat, combine the wine, 12.5 cl (4 fl oz) of water, the lemon juice, the remaining shallots, the remaining garlic and sage, and the remaining salt. Grind in a generous amount of pepper.

Rinse the fillets under cold running water, then cut them into bite-sized pieces. When the poaching liquid is hot, reduce the heat to low and place the fish in the liquid. Gently poach the fish for 5 minutes until the flesh just flakes.

Transfer the fish to a plate. Let it cool slightly, then refrigerate it. Do not discard the poaching liquid.

When the rice is done, refrigerate it in a large mixing bowl. Increase the heat to high and boil the poaching liquid for 5 minutes to reduce it slightly. Add the broad beans and tomatoes, and cook them for 3 minutes. Stir in the mange-tout and cook the mixture for 1 minute more, stirring constantly; there should be just 2 or 3 tablespoons of liquid remaining.

With a slotted spoon, transfer the vegetables to the bowl with the rice. Whisk the olive oil into the reduced liquid in the pan and pour this sauce over the rice and vegetables. Toss together well. Add the fish to the bowl and gently toss the salad once more. Serve at room temperature or chilled.

SUGGESTED ACCOMPANIMENT: *fruit salad.*

Indian-Spiced Monkfish

Serves 4
Working time: about 25 minutes
Total time: about 40 minutes

Calories **240**
Protein **22g**
Cholesterol **45mg**
Total fat **10g**
Saturated fat **1g**
Sodium **420mg**

500 g	*monkfish fillets*	*1 lb*
2	*lemons, juice only*	*2*
4	*garlic cloves, chopped*	*4*
1 tbsp	*chopped fresh ginger root*	*1 tbsp*
2 tbsp	*chopped fresh coriander*	*2 tbsp*
1 tsp	*coriander seeds*	*1 tsp*
1 tsp	*ground turmeric*	*1 tsp*
1 tsp	*dark brown sugar*	*1 tsp*
½ tsp	*cumin seeds*	*½ tsp*
¼ tsp	*mustard seeds*	*¼ tsp*
¼ tsp	*salt*	*¼ tsp*
2 tbsp	*safflower oil*	*2 tbsp*
1	*onion, finely chopped*	*1*
17.5 cl	*plain low-fat yogurt*	*6 fl oz*
75 g	*dry breadcrumbs*	*2½ oz*

In a blender, purée the lemon juice, garlic, ginger, coriander, coriander seeds, turmeric, brown sugar, cumin seeds, mustard seeds and salt. (Alternatively, grind the seasonings by hand in a mortar and pestle, then stir in the lemon juice.)

Heat 1 tablespoon of the oil in a heavy frying pan. Add the onion and cook it until it is translucent — about 4 minutes. Add the spice purée and cook for 3 minutes more. Remove the pan from the heat and set it aside.

Preheat the grill and preheat the oven to 230°C (450°F or Mark 8). Rinse the fish and pat it dry with paper towels. Slice the fillets crosswise into pieces about 5 cm (2 inches) wide.

Transfer the contents of the pan to a bowl and mix in the yogurt. Transfer half of this yogurt mixture to a small serving bowl and set it aside. Use the other half of the mixture to coat the fish: dip a piece of fish first in the yogurt, then in the breadcrumbs, covering it completely. Put the piece in a fireproof baking dish. Repeat ▶

the process with the remaining pieces.

Dribble the remaining oil over the fish. Grill the fish 7.5 cm (3 inches) below the heat source for about 3 minutes on each side. Transfer the dish to the oven and bake the fish until it feels firm to the touch — approximately 10 minutes. With a spatula, carefully remove the pieces from the baking dish. Serve the monkfish with the reserved yogurt sauce.

SUGGESTED ACCOMPANIMENT: *cucumber salad.*

Oven-Steamed Norway Haddock

Serves 6
Working time: about 10 minutes
Total time: about 50 minutes

Calories **235**
Protein **39g**
Cholesterol **160mg**
Total fat **8g**
Saturated fat **1g**
Sodium **180mg**

1.5 kg	*Norway haddock (or sea bass or sea trout), cleaned*	*3 lb*
2 tbsp	*dry sherry*	*2 tbsp*
2 tsp	*cornflour*	*2 tsp*
⅛ tsp	*salt*	*⅛ tsp*
5 cm	*piece of fresh ginger root, peeled and julienned*	*2 inch*
4	*spring onions, trimmed and cut into 5 cm (2 inch) pieces*	*4*
15 g	*fresh coriander leaves*	*½ oz*
2 tbsp	*low-sodium soy sauce or shoyu*	*2 tbsp*
1 tbsp	*Chinese black vinegar or balsamic vinegar*	*1 tbsp*
¼ tsp	*sugar*	*¼ tsp*

Combine the sherry, cornflour and salt in a small bowl. Rinse the fish under cold running water and pat it dry with paper towels. Cut four or five diagonal slashes on each side of the fish. Rub the sherry marinade over the fish, inside and out, working some of it into the slashes. Place the fish on the shiny side of a large piece of aluminium foil and let it marinate for at least 15 minutes.

Preheat the oven to 230°C (450°F or Mark 8). Insert a strip of ginger and a piece of spring onion into each slash. Place the remainder in the body cavity. Lay a few coriander leaves on top of the fish; put the remainder in the cavity. Combine the soy sauce, vinegar and sugar, and pour over the fish. Fold the foil over the fish and crimp the edges to seal the package tightly.

Set the foil package on a baking sheet and bake the fish until its flesh is opaque and feels firm to the touch — about 25 minutes. Carefully transfer the fish to a warmed serving platter. Pour over any liquid that has collected during baking, and serve immediately.

SUGGESTED ACCOMPANIMENTS: *stir-fried broccoli and water chestnuts; steamed rice.*

Redfish Creole

Serves 6
Working time: about 20 minutes
Total time: about 30 minutes

Calories **220**
Protein **21g**
Cholesterol **65mg**
Total fat **9g**
Saturated fat **3g**
Sodium **370mg**

600 g	*redfish fillets (or Norway haddock), the skin left on, cut into 6 equal pieces*	*1¼ lb*
20 g	*unsalted butter*	*¾ oz*
1	*small onion, coarsely chopped*	*1*
1	*sweet green pepper, seeded, deribbed and coarsely chopped*	*1*
1	*garlic clove, finely chopped*	*1*
750 g	*ripe tomatoes, skinned, seeded and coarsely chopped, or 400 g (14 oz) canned whole tomatoes, drained and coarsely chopped*	*1½ lb*
12.5 cl	*fish stock (recipe, page 136) or water*	*4 fl oz*
100 g	*okra, thinly sliced*	*3½ oz*
3 tbsp	*Dijon mustard*	*3 tbsp*
2 tbsp	*paprika, preferably Hungarian*	*2 tbsp*
½ tsp	*salt*	*½ tsp*
	freshly ground black pepper	
125 g	*cooked prawns, peeled and deveined*	*4 oz*
60 g	*flour*	*2 oz*
2 tbsp	*safflower oil*	*2 tbsp*

To prepare the sauce, first melt the butter in a saucepan over medium heat. Add the onion and green pepper; cook, stirring occasionally, until the onion becomes transparent and begins to turn golden — 4 to 5 minutes. Add the garlic and cook it, stirring, for 30 seconds. Stir in the tomatoes, stock or water, okra, mustard, paprika, ¼ teaspoon of the salt and some black pepper. Bring the mixture to the boil, reduce the heat to medium low and simmer the sauce for 5 minutes. Stir in the prawns and cook the sauce for 1 minute more. Set the saucepan aside.

Rinse the fillets under cold running water and pat them dry with paper towels. Season the fillets with the remaining salt and some black pepper. Place the fish in a polythene bag with the flour and shake the bag to coat the fillets.

Heat the oil in a large, heavy frying pan over medium-high heat. Sauté the fillets in the oil until they are opaque all the way through — approximately 2 minutes per side. Reheat the tomato sauce and pour it into a serving platter. Lay the fillets on top of the sauce and serve.

SUGGESTED ACCOMPANIMENT: *muffins or soft baps.*

Sea Trout Baked in Phyllo

Serves 6
Working time: about 45 minutes
Total time: about 1 hour 20 minutes

Calories **450**
Protein **32g**
Cholesterol **135mg**
Total fat **18g**
Saturated fat **4g**
Sodium **290mg**

1	*sea trout or salmon (about 2 kg/4 lb), filleted (page 130), the tail left attached to one of the fillets*	*1*
4 tbsp	*wild rice*	*4 tbsp*
35 cl	*fish stock (recipe, page 136) or water*	*12 fl oz*
¼ tsp	*fennel seeds*	*¼ tsp*
⅛ tsp	*salt*	*⅛ tsp*
90 g	*long-grain rice*	*3 oz*
2	*lemons, juice only of one, the other thinly sliced*	*2*
	freshly ground black pepper	
8	*sheets phyllo dough (about 75 g/3 oz)*	*8*
500 g	*asparagus, peeled, sliced diagonally into 2 cm (¾ inch) lengths and boiled for 2 minutes*	*1 lb*
1 tbsp	*safflower oil*	*1 tbsp*
1	*egg, beaten with 1 tsp water*	*1*
	Red-pepper sauce	
1 tbsp	*virgin olive oil*	*1 tbsp*
1	*garlic clove, crushed*	*1*
2	*sweet red peppers, seeded, deribbed and coarsely chopped*	*2*
12.5 cl	*fish stock (recipe, page 136) or unsalted chicken stock*	*4 fl oz*
½ tbsp	*white wine vinegar*	*½ tbsp*
⅛ tsp	*fennel seeds, crushed*	*⅛ tsp*
⅛ tsp	*salt*	*⅛ tsp*
⅛ tsp	*white pepper*	*⅛ tsp*

Preheat the oven to 180°C (350°F or Mark 4). Put the wild rice, stock or water, fennel seeds and salt in a small, fireproof casserole. Bring the liquid to the boil, then cover the pan tightly, and bake the wild rice in the oven for 25 minutes. Stir in the long-grain rice, return the pan to the oven and bake the mixed rice until all the liquid has been absorbed — 20 to 25 minutes more. Uncover the pan and allow the rice to cool before assembling the dish. Increase the oven temperature to 200°C (400°F or Mark 6).

Using tweezers or a small, sharp knife, remove any small bones from the fillets. Rinse the fillets under cold running water and pat them dry. Dribble the juice of one of the lemons over the fillets and grind some black pepper over them.

Transfer four stacked phyllo sheets to a baking sheet. Cover the remaining phyllo with a towel. Place on top of the stack the fillet that has the tail still attached, its skin side down. Spread a layer of rice over the fillet. Distribute the asparagus over the rice. Top the assembly with the second fillet, skin side up. Pat the remaining rice into the form of a fish head. Wrap the stacked phyllo around the trout and tuck the corners under the fish. Brush the entire assembly with the safflower oil.

Cut the remaining phyllo sheets into 10 strips, each 30 by 10 cm (12 by 4 inches). Fold each strip lengthwise into thirds. Lay a folded strip crosswise over the fish and tuck both ends under the bottom. Repeat the process with the remaining strips, overlapping them in evenly spaced ribbons from head to tail. With scissors, snip one edge of each ribbon at 1 cm (½ inch) intervals. Brush the ribbons lightly with the beaten egg.

Bake the fish until the pastry ribbons turn golden-brown — about 25 minutes.

Meanwhile, prepare the sauce. Heat the olive oil in a large frying pan over medium heat. Add the garlic and cook it for 1 minute, then add the peppers and cook them until they are soft — about 2 minutes more. Pour in the stock and vinegar, then stir in the fennel seeds, salt and white pepper. When the mixture simmers, remove it from the heat. Purée the mixture and strain it through a fine sieve into a sauceboat.

Transfer the fish to a serving platter and garnish it with the lemon slices. Let the fish cool for 5 minutes before slicing it. Serve with the sauce.

SUGGESTED ACCOMPANIMENT: *sliced fresh fennel.*

Almond-Sprinkled Mahimahi Stuffed with Chilies and Tomatoes

THE COLOURFUL MAHIMAHI, OR DOLPHIN FISH — A FISH, NOT A MAMMAL — IS CAUGHT IN SEMITROPICAL WATERS ON BOTH COASTS OF NORTH AMERICA AND IN THE MEDITERRANEAN.

Serves 6
Working time: about 40 minutes
Total time: about 1 hour

Calories **215**
Protein **23g**
Cholesterol **80mg**
Total fat **11g**
Saturated fat **3g**
Sodium **280mg**

750 g	*mahimahi fillet (or haddock)*	*1½ lb*
2 tbsp	*virgin olive oil*	*2 tbsp*
3	*garlic cloves, thinly sliced*	*3*
1 or 2	*small chili peppers, seeded and finely chopped (caution, page 45)*	*1 or 2*
1	*red onion, thinly sliced*	*1*
500 g	*ripe tomatoes, skinned, seeded and chopped*	*1 lb*
2	*lemons*	*2*
½ tsp	*salt*	*½ tsp*
45 g	*fresh parsley, coarsely chopped*	*1½ oz*
15 g	*unsalted butter*	*½ oz*
45 g	*almonds, sliced*	*1½ oz*

Rinse the fillet under cold running water and pat it dry with paper towels. With a sharp, thin-bladed knife, cut a large flap on one side of the centre line of the fillet: holding the knife parallel to the centre line at a flat angle, use short slicing strokes to cut from the middle towards the edge of the fillet. (Take care not to cut all the way through to the edge nor down to the bottom of the fillet.) Repeat the process to cut a flap on the other side of the centre line. Set the fish aside.

Preheat the oven to 240°C (475°F or Mark 9).

To prepare the stuffing, first pour the oil into a large, heavy frying pan over medium-high heat. Add the garlic and chili peppers and cook them for 30 seconds. Stir in the onion and cook for 2 minutes more. Add the tomatoes, the juice of one of the lemons and ¼ teaspoon of the salt. Cook the mixture, stirring often, until the tomatoes are very soft and almost all the liquid has evaporated — about 10 minutes.

While the stuffing mixture is cooking, cut six paper-thin slices from the remaining lemon and set them aside. Rub the juice from the remainder of the lemon over the outside of the fish and inside the flaps as well. Put the fish in a lightly oiled baking dish.

Stir the parsley into the tomato stuffing. Open the flaps on the fillet and fill the pocket with the stuffing.

Close over the flaps and arrange the lemon slices in a decorative pattern on top of the stuffing. Bake the fish in the oven until it is opaque and feels firm to the touch — 20 to 25 minutes.

Just before the fish is done, melt the butter in a small frying pan over medium heat. Add the sliced almonds and the remaining salt; toast the almonds, stirring constantly, until they are lightly browned — about 2 to 3 minutes. Remove the frying pan from the heat. Carefully transfer the baked fish to a warmed serving platter and scatter the almonds over the top. Serve immediately.

SUGGESTED ACCOMPANIMENT: *steamed rice.*

Fillets of Whiting with Mushroom Sauce

Serves 4
Working (and total) time: about 45 minutes

Calories **320**
Protein **35g**
Cholesterol **65mg**
Total fat **5g**
Saturated fat **2g**
Sodium **300mg**

4	*whiting (350 g/12 oz each), filleted and skinned (page 130)*	*4*
½ tsp	*salt*	*½ tsp*
	freshly ground black pepper	
3 tbsp	*lemon juice*	*3 tbsp*
30 cl	*fish stock (recipe, page 136)*	*½ pint*
250 g	*mushrooms, sliced thinly*	*8 oz*
15 g	*unsalted butter*	*½ oz*
15 g	*flour*	*½ oz*
2 tbsp	*single cream*	*2 tbsp*
750 g	*new potatoes, scrubbed*	*1½ lb*
2 tbsp	*chopped parsley*	*2 tbsp*

Rinse the fillets under cold running water and pat them dry with paper towels. Lay the fillets on a work surface skinned side up, season with half the salt, some pepper and 1 tablespoon of the lemon juice. Roll each fillet up from head to tail.

Place the fillets in a shallow saucepan, pour in the fish stock, cover the saucepan with a tightly fitting lid and cook gently for 8 to 10 minutes.

Meanwhile, put the potatoes on to boil. Place the sliced mushrooms in a bowl, add the remaining lemon juice and mix together.

Using a slotted spoon, lift the cooked whiting fillets from the saucepan on to paper towels to drain, then arrange neatly on a hot serving dish. Cover and keep warm while making the sauce.

Boil the fish stock rapidly until it is reduced to about ¼ litre (8 fl oz). Melt the butter in the saucepan, add the flour, then stir in the fish stock. Bring the liquid to the boil, stirring all the time. Add the sliced mushrooms and the remaining salt to the sauce, reduce the heat and simmer for 5 minutes until the mushrooms are softened. Stir the cream into the sauce and heat through for 1 minute.

When the potatoes are cooked but still firm, drain them and cut them into slices. Spoon the mushroom sauce over the whiting fillets, then garnish with the hot sliced potatoes and the chopped parsley.

Barbecued Swordfish with Chili Sauce

Serves 6
Working time: about 30 minutes
Total time: about 1 hour

Calories **265**
Protein **28g**
Cholesterol **55mg**
Total fat **9g**
Saturated fat **1g**
Sodium **325mg**

6	*small swordfish steaks (or cod), about 150 g (5 oz) each, 1 to 2 cm (½ to ¾ inch) thick*	*6*
2 tbsp	*fresh thyme, or 2 tsp dried thyme*	*2 tbsp*
3	*garlic cloves, finely chopped*	*3*
2	*lemons, juice only*	*2*
4	*large, dried mild chili peppers, stemmed and seeded (caution, page 45)*	*4*
30 g	*sun-dried tomatoes (3 or 4)*	*1 oz*
17.5 cl	*fish stock (recipe, page 136)*	*6 fl oz*
12.5 cl	*tawny port*	*4 fl oz*
2 tsp	*safflower oil*	*2 tsp*

Rinse the steaks under cold running water and pat them dry with paper towels. In a shallow dish large enough to hold the steaks in a single layer, combine the thyme, two thirds of the garlic and the lemon juice. Put the steaks in the dish and marinate them in the refrigerator for 1 hour, turning them once or twice.

Light the charcoal in the barbecue about 40 minutes before serving time. While the charcoal is heating, cover the chilies with 1 litre (1¾ pints) of boiling water and soak them for 20 minutes.

Drain the chilies and transfer them to a blender or food processor. Add the tomatoes and stock, and purée the mixture.

Pour the port into a non-reactive saucepan over medium-high heat; bring the port to the boil and cook it until it is reduced by half — 3 to 4 minutes. Stir in the chili-tomato purée and the remaining third of the garlic. Reduce the heat to medium and cook the sauce, stirring occasionally, for 5 minutes. Strain it through a fine sieve on to the bottom of a warm serving platter.

When the charcoal is hot, remove the steaks from the marinade and brush them with the oil. Cook the steaks for only 2 to 3 minutes per side — the flesh should be barely opaque. Set the steaks on top of the sauce and serve immediately.

SUGGESTED ACCOMPANIMENTS: *green salad; pitta bread.*

EDITOR'S NOTE: *If you wish to grill rather than barbecue the steaks, cook them for just 2 to 3 minutes per side.*

Grilled Swordfish in Apple-Tarragon Sauce

Serves 4
Working time: about 15 minutes
Total time: about 25 minutes

Calories **305**
Protein **30g**
Cholesterol **60mg**
Total fat **10g**
Saturated fat **2g**
Sodium **290mg**

750 g	*swordfish steak (or tuna), trimmed and cut into quarters*	*1½ lb*
2 tbsp	*safflower oil*	*2 tbsp*
2 tbsp	*finely chopped shallot*	*2 tbsp*
2 tbsp	*chopped fresh tarragon, or 2 tsp dried tarragon*	*2 tbsp*
12.5 cl	*fish stock (recipe, page 136)*	*4 fl oz*
4 tbsp	*unsweetened apple juice*	*4 tbsp*
1½ tsp	*cornflour, mixed with 1 tbsp cold water*	*1½ tsp*
¼ tsp	*salt*	*¼ tsp*
	freshly ground black pepper	
1	*red apple, quartered, cored and cut into thin wedges*	*1*
1	*yellow apple, quartered, cored and cut into thin wedges*	*1*

Preheat the grill or light the charcoal in the barbecue.

To prepare the sauce, pour 1 tablespoon of the oil into a saucepan over medium heat. Add the shallot and cook it until it is translucent — 1 to 2 minutes. Add the tarragon, stock, apple juice, cornflour mixture, ⅛ teaspoon of the salt and some pepper. Whisking constantly, bring the mixture to the boil and let it thicken. Reduce the heat to low and simmer the sauce for 2 to 3 minutes. Set the pan aside.

Rinse the fish steaks under cold running water and pat them dry with paper towels. Season the steaks with the remaining salt and a generous grinding of pepper, then brush them with the remaining oil. Grill or barbecue the steaks until their flesh is opaque and feels firm to the touch — 3 to 4 minutes per side.

When the fish is nearly done, reheat the sauce over low heat. Serve the steaks immediately, topped with the warm sauce and garnished with the apple slices.

SUGGESTED ACCOMPANIMENT: *sautéed yellow squash or courgettes with chopped spring onion tops.*

Grayling Gratin

Serves 6
Working time: about 40 minutes
Total time: about 1 hour and 10 minutes

Calories **300**
Protein **19g**
Cholesterol **45mg**
Total fat **9g**
Saturated fat **3g**
Sodium **170mg**

500 g	*skinned grayling fillets (or other white fish)*	*1 lb*
1	*lemon, juice only*	*1*
	freshly ground black pepper	
1 kg	*waxy potatoes, scrubbed*	*2 lb*
1.25 kg	*ripe tomatoes, quartered, or 800 g (28 oz) canned whole tomatoes, chopped, juice reserved*	*2½ lb*
1	*fresh hot green chili pepper, seeded and chopped (caution, page 45)*	*1*
2	*garlic cloves, finely chopped*	*2*
1 tsp	*chopped fresh oregano, or ½ tsp dried oregano*	*1 tsp*
¼ tsp	*ground cumin*	*¼ tsp*
¼ tsp	*cayenne pepper*	*¼ tsp*
¼ tsp	*salt*	*¼ tsp*
1 tbsp	*virgin olive oil*	*1 tbsp*
2	*onions, thinly sliced*	*2*
	Herbed topping	
45 g	*dry breadcrumbs*	*1½ oz*
2 tbsp	*chopped fresh parsley*	*2 tbsp*
¼ tsp	*chopped fresh oregano, or ⅛ tsp dried oregano*	*¼ tsp*
⅛ tsp	*ground cumin*	*⅛ tsp*
20 g	*unsalted butter*	*¾ oz*

Rinse the fish fillets under cold running water and pat them dry with paper towels. Put them on a plate and dribble the lemon juice over them. Season the fillets with a liberal grinding of black pepper and set them aside while you prepare the potatoes.

Put the potatoes in a saucepan, pour in enough water to cover them by about 2.5 cm (1 inch) and bring the water to the boil. Reduce the heat to medium and cook the potatoes until they are tender when pierced with a fork — about 15 minutes.

While the potatoes are cooking, prepare the sauce. Put the fresh tomatoes in a large wide pan with 12.5 cl (4 fl oz) of water. (If you are using canned tomatoes, add their juice but no water.) Cook the tomatoes over medium heat, stirring frequently, until they are very soft and most of the liquid has evaporated — about 20 minutes. Purée the tomatoes by working them through a sieve. Combine the tomato purée with the green chili, garlic, oregano, cumin, cayenne pepper and salt.

Heat the oil in a large, heavy frying pan over medium-high heat. Add the onions and cook them,

stirring constantly, until they are a golden-brown and quite soft — about 7 minutes. Add 12.5 cl (4 fl oz) of water to the onions to deglaze the pan; stir well and set the pan aside.

Preheat the oven to 230°C (450°F or Mark 8). When the potatoes are cool enough to handle, peel them and cut them into chunks. In a large baking dish, mix the potatoes with the tomato sauce and the onions. Carefully place the fillets on top of the potato mixture.

To prepare the topping, combine the breadcrumbs, parsley, oregano and cumin. Sprinkle the topping over the fillets, covering them completely. Cut the butter into small pieces and scatter them over the topping. Bake the dish until the fish feels firm to the touch — 15 to 20 minutes, depending on the fillets' thickness.

SUGGESTED ACCOMPANIMENT: *spinach salad.*

Skate with Red Pepper and French Beans

Serves 4
Working (and total) time: about 40 minutes

Calories **325**
Protein **31g**
Cholesterol **60mg**
Total fat **10g**
Saturated fat **1g**
Sodium **275mg**

1 kg	*skate wings, skinned*	*2 lb*
½ litre	*dry white wine*	*16 fl oz*
¼ litre	*fish stock (recipe, page 136) or water*	*8 fl oz*
1	*shallot, thinly sliced*	*1*
2	*fresh thyme sprigs, or ¾ tsp dried thyme*	*2*
8	*whole cloves*	*8*
4	*spring onions, trimmed and thinly sliced, white parts kept separate from the green*	*4*
4 tbsp	*red wine vinegar*	*4 tbsp*
2 tbsp	*virgin olive oil*	*2 tbsp*
1 tbsp	*fresh lemon juice*	*1 tbsp*
1	*sweet red pepper, seeded, deribbed and thinly sliced*	*1*
¼ tsp	*salt*	*¼ tsp*
	freshly ground black pepper	
150 g	*French beans, trimmed, halved lengthwise diagonally*	*5 oz*

Rinse the skate well under cold running water. In a large, non-reactive frying pan, combine the wine, the stock or water, the shallot, thyme and cloves. Bring the mixture to the boil, then reduce the heat to medium-low and put the skate in the liquid. Poach the fish until it is opaque — about 12 minutes.

While the skate is cooking, prepare the vinaigrette: combine the white spring onion slices, the vinegar, oil and lemon juice in a large bowl. Set the vinaigrette aside.

When the skate is cooked, transfer it to a plate. Strain the poaching liquid into a bowl, then pour the strained liquid back into the pan. Add the pepper strips, the salt and some pepper, and cook over medium-low heat for 5 minutes. Add the beans to the pan; cook the vegetables for 5 minutes more.

With a slotted spoon, transfer the vegetables to the bowl containing the vinaigrette. Stir the green spring onion slices into the vegetable mixture. Increase the heat under the pan to high and boil the liquid rapidly until it is syrupy — 2 to 3 minutes. Pour the liquid into the vegetable mixture.

With your fingers, lift the skate meat from the cartilage. Put the meat on a serving platter and arrange the vegetables around it, spooning some of the vinaigrette over the top. Serve warm or cold.

EDITOR'S NOTE: *If the skate wings have not been skinned beforehand, slip a sharp, thin-bladed knife between the skin and the flesh. Pressing the knife against the flesh and working towards the edge of the wing, cut away the skin with short slicing strokes. Turn the wing over and repeat the process to remove the skin from the other side.*

Red Snapper in Saffron Sauce

Serves 4
Working (and total) time: about 30 minutes

Calories **245**
Protein **24g**
Cholesterol **80mg**
Total fat **9g**
Saturated fat **4g**
Sodium **200mg**

500 g	*skinned red snapper fillets (or John Dory)*	*1 lb*
¼ tsp	*salt*	*¼ tsp*
¼ litre	*dry white wine*	*8 fl oz*
1	*shallot, chopped*	*1*
1	*garlic clove, crushed*	*1*
1	*fresh thyme sprig, or ½ tsp dried thyme*	*1*
1 tsp	*fennel seeds, crushed*	*1 tsp*
10	*black peppercorns, cracked*	*10*
15 g	*unsalted butter*	*½ oz*
20	*saffron threads, steeped in 4 tbsp hot water for 10 minutes*	*20*
1 tsp	*Dijon mustard*	*1 tsp*
4 tbsp	*single cream, mixed with ½ tsp cornflour*	*4 tbsp*

Gently rinse the fillets under cold running water and pat them dry with paper towels. Sprinkle the fish with the salt and set it aside.

In a large, heavy frying pan, combine the wine, shallot, garlic, thyme, fennel seeds, peppercorns and butter. Bring the mixture to the boil, then reduce the heat to medium and simmer for 3 minutes. Put the fillets in the liquid and reduce the heat to low. Cover the pan and poach the fish until it is opaque and feels firm to the touch — about 6 minutes. Carefully transfer the fish to a warmed serving dish and cover the fish with aluminium foil to keep it warm.

Increase the heat under the pan to medium-high and reduce the poaching liquid to approximately 12.5 cl (4 fl oz) — about 5 minutes. Strain the liquid into a small saucepan. Pour into the saucepan any juices that have collected on the serving dish, then stir in the saffron mixture and the mustard. Simmer the sauce for 2 minutes. Whisk in the cream-and-cornflour mixture, and cook the sauce until it thickens slightly — about 1 minute more. Pour round the fillets and serve at once.

SUGGESTED ACCOMPANIMENT: *boiled new potatoes.*

Stir-Fried Shark with Chinese Cabbage

Serves 4
Working time: about 15 minutes
Total time: about 30 minutes

Calories **240**
Protein **25g**
Cholesterol **45mg**
Total fat **9g**
Saturated fat **1g**
Sodium **355mg**

500 g	*shark meat (or swordfish or tuna)*	*1 lb*
2 tbsp	*low-sodium soy sauce or shoyu*	*2 tbsp*
1 tbsp	*dark sesame oil*	*1 tbsp*
1 tbsp	*fresh lime juice*	*1 tbsp*
1	*bunch spring onions, trimmed, sliced diagonally into 1 cm (½ inch) pieces, the white parts kept separate from the green*	*1*
2	*garlic cloves, finely chopped*	*2*
1 tbsp	*orange marmalade or apricot jam*	*1 tbsp*
	freshly ground black pepper	
1½ tbsp	*safflower oil*	*1½ tbsp*
1	*carrot, peeled, halved lengthwise and cut diagonally into thin slices*	*1*
500 g	*Chinese cabbage, trimmed and sliced into 2 cm (¾ inch) strips*	*1 lb*

Wash the fish under cold running water and pat it dry with paper towels. Cut it into pieces about 5 cm (2 inches) long and 1 cm (½ inch) wide. In a large bowl, combine 1 tablespoon of the soy sauce with the sesame oil, lime juice, white spring onion pieces, garlic, marmalade or jam and some pepper. Add the fish pieces to the mixture and let them marinate for at least 15 minutes.

In a wok or a large frying pan, heat 1 tablespoon of the safflower oil over high heat. Add the carrot slices and stir-fry them for 1 minute, then add the cabbage, all but 1 tablespoon of the green spring onion pieces and the remaining soy sauce. Stir-fry the vegetables until the cabbage is barely wilted — about 2 minutes. Transfer the vegetables to a bowl.

Heat the remaining safflower oil in the wok or pan over high heat. Add the marinated fish and gently stir-fry it until it is opaque and feels firm to the touch — approximately 2 minutes. Return the vegetables to the pan and toss them with the fish. Transfer the mixture to a large plate, sprinkle with the reserved green spring onion pieces, and serve.

SUGGESTED ACCOMPANIMENT: *fresh Chinese egg noodles.*

Prosciutto-Stuffed Plaice Fillets with Hot-and-Sour Sauce

Serves 4
Working time: about 30 minutes
Total time: about 1 hour

Calories **145**
Protein **21g**
Cholesterol **55mg**
Total fat **3g**
Saturated fat **1g**
Sodium **345mg**

4	*plaice or sole fillets (about 125 g/4 oz each)*	4
2 tbsp	*rice wine or dry white wine*	2 tbsp
4	*spring onions, trimmed, the bottom 7.5 cm (3 inches) halved lengthwise, the tops thinly sliced diagonally*	4
8	*mange-tout, strings removed and halved lengthwise*	8
½	*sweet red pepper, seeded, deribbed and cut lengthwise into thin strips*	½
1	*paper-thin slice of prosciutto or other dry-cured ham (about 15 g/½ oz), cut into 8 thin strips*	1
	Hot-and-sour sauce	
1	*lemon*	1
1 tbsp	*rice vinegar*	1 tbsp
1 tbsp	*low-sodium soy sauce or shoyu*	1 tbsp
1 tsp	*sweet chili sauce, or ½ tsp crushed dried red chili pepper mixed with 1 tsp golden syrup and ½ tsp vinegar*	1 tsp
¼ tsp	*dark sesame oil*	¼ tsp
1 tsp	*cornflour, mixed with 2 tsp water*	1 tsp
1 tsp	*safflower oil*	1 tsp
1 tbsp	*grated fresh ginger root*	1 tbsp
1	*garlic clove, finely chopped*	1

Rinse the fillets under cold running water and pat them dry with paper towels. Put the fillets in a shallow dish

and sprinkle them with the wine; let the fish marinate in the refrigerator for 30 minutes.

At the end of the marinating time, blanch the spring onion bottoms and mange-tout in boiling water for 10 seconds. (The pepper strips do not need blanching.) Drain and refresh them under cold water. Drain the wine from the fillets and discard it; pat the fillets dry.

Lay one quarter of the spring onion bottoms, mange-tout and red pepper and two strips of prosciutto across the centre of a fillet. Roll up the fillet and place it seam side down on a plate. Roll up the remaining fillets and vegetables and set each roll on the plate. Set the plate in a bamboo steamer basket and put the basket in a wok or large frying pan filled 2.5 cm (1 inch) deep with water. (If you lack such a steamer, set the plate on a flat wire rack in the bottom of a large saucepan or frying pan filled about 1 cm/½ inch deep with water.) Cover tightly and steam the fish rolls until the flesh is opaque — about 6 minutes.

Meanwhile, make the hot-and-sour sauce. Grate the rind of the lemon into a small bowl. Squeeze the lemon juice into the bowl and add the vinegar, soy sauce, sweet chili sauce, dark sesame oil and cornflour. Stir the mixture thoroughly. Heat the safflower oil in a small, heavy-bottomed pan over medium heat. Add the ginger and garlic and cook for 2 minutes, taking care not to let the garlic brown. Stir in the vinegar mixture and cook for about 1 minute to thicken slightly.

When the fish rolls are done, drain the accumulated liquid on the plate into the sauce; stir the sauce well to incorporate the liquid. Carefully transfer the fish rolls to individual plates. Pour the sauce over them and garnish with the spring onion tops. Serve immediately.

SUGGESTED ACCOMPANIMENT: *cellophane noodles tossed with dark sesame oil.*

Halibut Steaks in Peppery Papaya Sauce

Serves 4
Working time: about 25 minutes
Total time: about 40 minutes

Calories **275**
Protein **28g**
Cholesterol **80mg**
Total fat **13g**
Saturated fat **5g**
Sodium **240mg**

4	*halibut steaks, total weight 750 g (1½ lb)*	*4*
1 tbsp	*safflower oil*	*1 tbsp*
1	*papaya (about 500 g/1 lb), peeled, seeded and cut into 2.5 cm (1 inch) pieces*	*1*
1	*small onion, coarsely chopped*	*1*
¼ tsp	*salt*	*¼ tsp*
12.5 cl	*fish stock (recipe, page 136)*	*4 fl oz*
6 tbsp	*fresh lime juice*	*6 tbsp*
3 tbsp	*double cream*	*3 tbsp*
½	*large, dried mild chili pepper, seeded and sliced into paper-thin strips (caution, page 45), or ¾ tsp red pepper flakes*	*½*
2	*spring onions, trimmed and sliced diagonally into 1 cm (½ inch) pieces*	*2*

Heat the oil in a large, non-reactive frying pan over medium heat. Add the papaya, onion and ⅛ teaspoon of the salt. Cook the mixture, stirring frequently, for 7 minutes. Pour in the stock and all but 1 tablespoon of the lime juice. Bring the liquid to the boil, reduce the heat to low, and simmer the mixture, partially covered, for 10 minutes. Preheat the grill.

Transfer the papaya mixture to a food processor or blender. Purée the mixture until it is smooth, stopping once to scrape down the sides. Put the cream and the chili pepper or red pepper flakes in a non-reactive saucepan over medium heat. Simmer the cream for 3 minutes, whisking occasionally. Reduce the heat to low and whisk the papaya purée into the cream a spoonful at a time.

Rinse the steaks under cold running water and pat them dry with paper towels. Sprinkle the fish with the remaining salt and the remaining lime juice. Put the steaks in a lightly-buttered shallow, fireproof dish and grill them about 10 cm (4 inches) below the heat source for 4 minutes on the first side. Turn them over, sprinkle them with the sliced spring onions, and continue cooking until the flesh feels firm to the touch and the spring onions are browned — approximately 3 minutes.

Transfer the steaks to a warmed platter and spoon the papaya sauce round them. Serve immediately.

SUGGESTED ACCOMPANIMENT: *rice salad.*

Poached Halibut with Avocado Sauce

Serves 4
Working (and total) time: about 30 minutes

Calories **310**
Protein **36g**
Cholesterol **95mg**
Total fat **18g**
Saturated fat **2g**
Sodium **255mg**

4	*halibut steaks (about 250 g/8 oz each)*	*4*
60 cl	*court-bouillon (recipe, page 136)*	*1 pint*
	Avocado sauce	
1	*large ripe avocado*	*1*
2 tbsp	*fresh lime juice*	*2 tbsp*
½	*small fresh green chili pepper, seeded and chopped (caution, page 45)*	*½*
¼ tsp	*salt*	*¼ tsp*
	freshly ground black pepper	
	Garnish	
1	*small lemon, thinly sliced*	*1*
1	*lime, thinly sliced*	*1*
	fresh parsley sprigs (optional)	

Trim the halibut steaks to neaten, then rinse them under cold water. Pat them dry with paper towels.

Pour the court-bouillon into a wide shallow saucepan or fireproof casserole. Place the halibut steaks in the court-bouillon in a single layer, ensuring that they are well covered with liquid. Cover the saucepan and simmer the halibut for 6 to 8 minutes, until the flesh flakes easily.

Meanwhile, cut the avocado in half lengthwise and remove the stone. Carefully peel away the skin, then roughly chop the flesh. Place the avocado in a food processor or blender with the lime juice, chili pepper, salt and pepper. Blend for 1 minute until very smooth. (Alternatively, the ingredients may be mashed together in a mixing bowl with a fork.) Spoon the sauce into a serving bowl and set aside.

Using a slotted spoon, carefully lift the halibut steaks out of the court-bouillon on to a hot serving dish. Garnish with the sliced lemon and lime and the parsley sprigs, if using. Serve immediately, accompanied by the avocado sauce.

SUGGESTED ACCOMPANIMENT: *new potatoes tossed in chives.*

Flounder-Stuffed Tomatoes

Serves 6 as an appetizer
Working time: about 35 minutes
Total time: about 45 minutes

Calories **155**
Protein **15g**
Cholesterol **45mg**
Total fat **7g**
Saturated fat **2g**
Sodium **200mg**

500 g	*flounder fillets (or plaice or sole)*	*1 lb*
6	*large ripe tomatoes*	*6*
3	*carrots, peeled and thinly sliced*	*3*
2 tbsp	*fresh lemon juice*	*2 tbsp*
1½ tbsp	*virgin olive oil*	*1½ tbsp*
5	*garlic cloves, crushed*	*5*
1	*large shallot, chopped*	*1*
1 tsp	*fresh thyme, or ¼ tsp dried thyme*	*1 tsp*
¼ tsp	*salt*	*¼ tsp*
	freshly ground black pepper	
4 tbsp	*single cream*	*4 tbsp*

Rinse the fillets under cold running water and pat them dry with paper towels. Slice the fillets crosswise into pieces about 1 cm (½ inch) wide.

Slice the tops off the tomatoes and reserve them. With a spoon, scoop out and discard the seeds and juice. Set the tomatoes upside down on paper towels to drain. Preheat the oven to 200°C (400°F or Mark 6).

Cook the carrots in boiling water with the lemon juice until they are quite soft — about 15 minutes.

While the carrots are cooking, heat the oil in a large, heavy frying pan over medium heat. Add the garlic cloves and cook them for 2 minutes. Stir in the shallot and cook it for 30 seconds. Add the fish pieces, the thyme, ⅛ teaspoon of the salt and a generous grinding of pepper. Cook the mixture for 10 minutes, stirring gently with a fork to break up the fish. Stir in the cream and remove the frying pan from the heat. Discard the cloves of garlic.

When the carrots are done, drain them, reserving 6 tablespoons of the cooking liquid. In a food processor, blender or sieve, purée the carrots, reserved cooking liquid, the remaining salt and some pepper until smooth. Add the carrot purée to the pan and mix gently; spoon the mixture into the tomato shells.

Put the filled tomato shells on a baking sheet or in a baking dish and cover them with the reserved tops. Bake the shells until their skin starts to crack — about 10 minutes. Remove the shells from the oven and discard the tops. Serve at once.

Seviche of Plaice

SEVICHE IS A SPANISH WORD FOR RAW FISH "COOKED" IN AN ACIDIC MARINADE. SO THAT THE FISH WILL BE THE FRESHEST POSSIBLE, THE BONING AND FILLETING SHOULD BE DONE JUST BEFORE THE DISH IS ASSEMBLED.

Serves 6 as an appetizer
Working time: about 30 minutes
Total time: about 3 hours and 30 minutes

Calories **110**
Protein **15g**
Cholesterol **40mg**
Total fat **1g**
Saturated fat **0g**
Sodium **170mg**

1.5 kg	*whole plaice (or sole), boned and filleted, yielding about 500 g (1 lb) of fillets*	*3 lb*
4	*lemons, halved, the juice and 6 of the empty halves reserved*	*4*
5	*limes, juice only*	*5*
12.5 cl	*fresh orange juice*	*4 fl oz*
3	*hot chili peppers, halved, seeded and thinly sliced crosswise (caution, page 45)*	*3*
2 tbsp	*chopped fresh coriander or parsley*	*2 tbsp*
1	*garlic clove, finely chopped*	*1*
2 tbsp	*sugar*	*2 tbsp*
¼ tsp	*salt*	*¼ tsp*
	freshly ground black pepper	
18	*lettuce leaves, washed and dried*	*18*
1	*small red onion, thinly sliced, the rings separated*	*1*

Rinse the fillets under cold running water and pat them dry with paper towels. Cut the fillets into bite-sized strips about 6 cm (2½ inches) long and 2.5 cm (1 inch) wide; then arrange the fish strips in a single layer in a shallow 20 by 28 cm (8 by 11 inch) glass dish.

In a separate bowl, combine all of the remaining ingredients except the reserved lemon halves, the lettuce and onion. Stir the mixture well and pour it over the fish to just cover. If necessary, add more lemon juice. Cover and refrigerate until the thickest piece of fish, when cut in half, is opaque throughout — about 3 hours.

Cut the edge of each reserved lemon half in a decorative sawtooth pattern. To serve the seviche, spoon some of it into each lemon half. Divide the lettuce between six serving plates. Set a filled lemon half and some of the remaining seviche on the lettuce on each plate, and garnish with the onion rings.

Sole Baked in Parchment

Serves 4
Working time: about 15 minutes
Total time: about 30 minutes

Calories **170**
Protein **20g**
Cholesterol **70mg**
Total fat **8g**
Saturated fat **4g**
Sodium **275mg**

4	*sole or plaice fillets, about 125 g (4 oz) each*	*4*
2	*small courgettes (preferably 1 green and 1 yellow), thinly sliced*	*2*
3	*large mushrooms, thinly sliced*	*3*
4	*fresh thyme sprigs, or ½ tsp dried thyme*	*4*
4 tbsp	*dry vermouth or dry white wine*	*4 tbsp*
30 g	*unsalted butter, cut into small pieces*	*1 oz*
¼ tsp	*salt*	*¼ tsp*
	freshly ground black pepper	

Preheat the oven to 220°C (425°F or Mark 7). Rinse the fillets under cold running water and pat them dry with paper towels. Using a diagonal lengthwise cut, divide each fillet in half to make one thick and one thin fillet.

Cut four pieces of parchment paper or aluminium foil about 30 by 45 cm (12 by 18 inches). Fold each piece in half lengthwise, then cut each piece into a half-heart shape, as you would a valentine. Flatten out and lightly butter each heart.

Layer one quarter of the fish and vegetables on one half of a heart. Begin with a bed of courgette (but save enough to form a top layer). Place a thick fillet on the courgette bed; top the fillet with the mushrooms. Put a thin fillet on top of the mushrooms, and top it in turn with a final layer of the reserved courgette. To each layered assembly, add a sprig of fresh thyme or a sprinkling of dried thyme, 1 tablespoon of the vermouth or wine, one quarter of the butter, one quarter of the salt and some pepper.

Fold the other half of the heart over the layered assembly and bring the cut edges together. Seal the package by crimping the cut edges together in a series of small, neat folds.

Transfer the packages to a baking sheet. Bake them for 10 minutes per 2.5 cm (1 inch) of thickness of the entire assembly — approximately 15 minutes in all.

Put the packages on individual plates; let each diner open his own package.

SUGGESTED ACCOMPANIMENT: *pitta bread.*

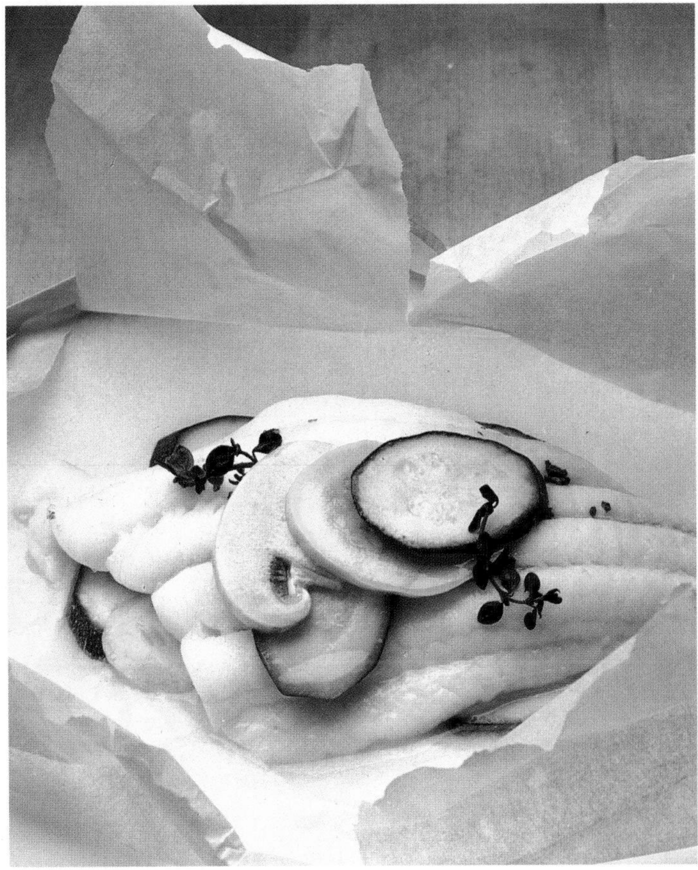

Prawns and Asparagus Wrapped in Sole

Serves 6
Working (and total) time: about 1 hour

Calories **200**
Protein **21g**
Cholesterol **90mg**
Total fat **5g**
Saturated fat **2g**
Sodium **125mg**

3	*sole (or plaice), about 600 to 750 g (1¼ to 1½ lb) each*	3
35 cl	*dry white wine*	12 fl oz
1 tbsp	*red wine vinegar*	1 tbsp
250 g	*medium prawns, peeled and deveined, the shells reserved*	8 oz
150 g	*asparagus, sliced diagonally into 5 mm (¼ inch) pieces*	5 oz
2 tbsp	*finely cut fresh dill*	2 tbsp
3	*shallots, finely chopped*	3
1½ tbsp	*fresh lemon juice*	1½ tbsp
	freshly ground black pepper	
3	*ripe tomatoes, skinned, seeded and coarsely chopped*	3
2 tsp	*tomato paste*	2 tsp
20 g	*cold unsalted butter, cut into small pieces*	¾ oz

Pour the wine, vinegar and ¼ litre (8 fl oz) of water into a large, non-reactive saucepan over medium heat. Add the reserved prawn shells and simmer them for 20 minutes to obtain an aromatic liquid.

While the shells are simmering, fillet the fish as demonstrated on page 131 (you will have six longer, thicker fillets and six shorter, thinner fillets). Rinse the fillets under cold running water, pat them dry with paper towels, and set them aside.

Strain the prawn-shell liquid through a sieve, pushing down on the shells so that they release every bit of flavour. Discard the shells and pour the liquid back into the saucepan over medium heat. Add the prawns and asparagus, and blanch them for 30 seconds. Remove the pan from the heat. With a slotted spoon, transfer the prawns and asparagus to a large bowl. (Do not discard the liquid — it will serve as the base for the sauce.) Add 1 tablespoon of the dill, half of the shallots, the lemon juice and some pepper to the bowl; mix well and set the bowl aside.

Preheat the oven to 190°C (375°F or Mark 5). Lightly oil a baking dish. With a diagonal crosswise cut, slice one of the thinner fish fillets in half at the middle. Overlap the two halves to form a base for the assembly, and set the base in the baking dish. Wrap a larger fillet around the base to form a collar with the two ends meeting, and pin the ends together with a toothpick. Fill the resulting shape with one sixth of the prawn and asparagus mixture. Repeat the process with the remaining fillets and filling to form six portions.

Lightly cover the dish with aluminium foil, its dull side up. Bake until the sole is opaque and the prawns and asparagus are hot — about 15 minutes.

While the fish is baking, prepare the sauce. Add the tomatoes, tomato paste and the remaining shallots to the liquid in the saucepan, and set the pan over medium-high heat. Cook the sauce, stirring often, until it is reduced to about 30 cl (½ pint) — about 10 minutes. Purée the sauce in a food processor or blender. Return it to the pan and stir in the remaining dill. Keep the sauce warm over low heat.

When the fish is done, carefully transfer each portion to a warmed serving platter and remove the toothpicks. Whisk the butter into the sauce along with a grinding of black pepper. Pour some of the sauce around the fish and pass the rest separately.

SUGGESTED ACCOMPANIMENT: *saffron rice.*

Brill with Curried Tomato Sauce

Serves 4
Working time: about 20 minutes
Total time: about 50 minutes

Calories **195**
Protein **23g**
Cholesterol **60mg**
Total fat **6g**
Saturated fat **1g**
Sodium **215mg**

4	*brill fillets (or halibut), about 125 g (4 oz) each, rinsed and patted dry*	4
1	*shallot, finely chopped*	1
1	*garlic clove, finely chopped*	1
⅛ tsp	*salt*	⅛ tsp
	freshly ground black pepper	
1 tbsp	*dry white wine*	1 tbsp
6 tbsp	*fish stock (recipe, page 136) or water*	6 tbsp
	parsley sprigs	
	Curried tomato sauce	
1 tbsp	*virgin olive oil*	1 tbsp
2	*garlic cloves, finely chopped*	2
2 tsp	*curry powder*	2 tsp
1.25 kg	*ripe tomatoes, skinned, seeded and finely chopped*	2½ lb
⅛ tsp	*salt*	⅛ tsp
	freshly ground black pepper	
2 tsp	*tomato paste*	2 tsp
1 tbsp	*chopped fresh parsley*	1 tbsp

To make the sauce, heat the oil in a large, heavy-bottomed saucepan over low heat. Add the garlic and stir until it is soft but not browned — about 30 seconds. Sprinkle in the curry powder and cook for 30 seconds more, stirring constantly. Stir in the tomatoes, salt and some pepper, and simmer until the tomatoes are very soft — about 30 minutes. Add the tomato paste, then purée the sauce, return it to the pan, and set it aside.

Preheat the oven to 220°C (425°F or Mark 7). Lightly oil the bottom of a heavy, shallow baking dish. Cut a piece of parchment paper or aluminium foil to the dimensions of the dish, and lightly oil one side of it.

Sprinkle the chopped shallot and garlic into the baking dish. Fold the fillets in half, arrange them in the dish and sprinkle them with the salt and some pepper. Pour the wine and the stock or water over the fish. Lay the parchment paper or foil, oiled side down, over the fish. Bake the fillets until their flesh is opaque — approximately 9 minutes.

Remove the parchment paper or foil and set it aside. With two fish slices, carefully transfer the fillets to a warmed serving platter. Re-cover the fillets with the parchment paper or foil and keep them warm. Strain the cooking liquid through a fine sieve into the reserved tomato sauce. Bring the sauce to the boil and cook it, stirring, until it thickens — about 2 minutes. Stir in the chopped parsley.

Spoon the sauce around the fish fillets and garnish them with the parsley sprigs. Serve immediately, with the remaining sauce on the side.

SUGGESTED ACCOMPANIMENT: *julienned courgettes.*

Cod Steaks Cooked with Green Pepper and Tomatoes

Serves 4
Working time: about 20 minutes
Total time: about 50 minutes

Calories **195**
Protein **32g**
Cholesterol **70mg**
Total fat **5g**
Saturated fat **1g**
Sodium **340mg**

4	*cod steaks (175 to 250 g/6 to 8 oz each)*	4
1 tbsp	*virgin olive oil*	1 tbsp
1	*onion, halved and sliced thinly*	1
1	*large sweet green pepper, seeded, deribbed and sliced thinly*	1
500 g	*tomatoes, skinned, seeded and chopped*	1 lb
3	*garlic cloves, crushed*	3
2 tsp	*mixed fresh herbs (thyme, oregano and rosemary)*	2 tsp
½ tsp	*salt*	½ tsp
	freshly ground black pepper	

Garnish
fresh thyme sprigs
black olives

Trim the fins from the cod steaks to neaten. Rinse under cold running water, then pat dry with paper towels. Preheat the oven to 200°C (400°F or Mark 6).

Heat the oil in a large frying pan, add the cod steaks and brown them very lightly on both sides. Transfer them to a shallow ovenproof dish.

Add the onion and pepper to the oil remaining in the frying pan. Sauté them gently until softened but not browned. Stir the tomatoes, garlic, herbs and seasoning into the onion and pepper.

Spoon the pepper and tomato mixture over the cod steaks. Cover the dish and cook in the oven for 30 to 35 minutes, until the cod flakes easily.

Garnish the steaks with sprigs of fresh thyme and black olives. Serve immediately.

Cod Fishcakes with Horseradish Sauce

Serves 4
Working time: about 20 minutes
Total time: about 40 minutes

Calories **180**
Protein **21g**
Cholesterol **105mg**
Total fat **4g**
Saturated fat **1g**
Sodium **490mg**

350 g	*cod fillets (or haddock or coley)*	*12 oz*
125 g	*dry breadcrumbs*	*4 oz*
1	*egg*	*1*
1	*egg white*	*1*
125 g	*onion, finely chopped*	*4 oz*
4 tbsp	*chopped parsley or fresh coriander*	*4 tbsp*
3	*garlic cloves, finely chopped*	*3*
2 tbsp	*grainy mustard*	*2 tbsp*
2 tbsp	*anise-flavoured liqueur (optional)*	*2 tbsp*
2 tbsp	*fresh lemon juice*	*2 tbsp*
1½ tsp	*capers, drained and chopped*	*1½ tsp*
1 tbsp	*paprika*	*1 tbsp*
¼ tsp	*cayenne pepper*	*¼ tsp*
15 cl	*plain low-fat yogurt*	*¼ pint*
2 tbsp	*red wine vinegar*	*2 tbsp*
1 tsp	*prepared horseradish*	*1 tsp*

Preheat the oven to 200°C (400°F or Mark 6). With a large knife, finely chop the fish. Put the fish in a large mixing bowl. Add 45 g (1½ oz) of the breadcrumbs, the egg, egg white, onion, all but 1 tablespoon of the parsley or coriander, the garlic, 1 tablespoon of the mustard, the liqueur if you are using it, the lemon juice, capers, paprika and cayenne pepper, and mix thoroughly.

Put the remaining breadcrumbs in a shallow bowl. Divide the fish mixture into eight equal portions. Pat one of the portions into a cake about 2 cm (¾ inch) thick. Coat the cake well with breadcrumbs and place it on an oiled baking sheet. Repeat these steps to form the remaining portions into crumbed fishcakes. Bake the fishcakes for 20 minutes.

While the fishcakes are in the oven, prepare the sauce in a small bowl, mix the remaining mustard and the remaining parsley or coriander with the yogurt, the vinegar and the horseradish.

Serve the fishcakes with a dollop of sauce on the side.

SUGGESTED ACCOMPANIMENT: *red cabbage salad.*

Baked Cod Plaki

PLAKI IS A GREEK FISH DISH BAKED ON A BED OF TOMATOES.

Serves 6
Working time: about 30 minutes
Total time: about 45 minutes

Calories **150**
Protein **17g**
Cholesterol **50mg**
Total fat **5g**
Saturated fat **3g**
Sodium **350mg**

500 g	*cod fillets (or haddock, halibut or coley)*	*1 lb*
2	*large ripe tomatoes, sliced*	*2*
2	*small onions, sliced*	*2*
1	*fennel bulb, cored, sliced crosswise, feathery tops reserved*	*1*
2	*garlic cloves, finely chopped*	*2*
1 tbsp	*chopped fresh oregano, or 2 tsp dried oregano*	*1 tbsp*
3 tbsp	*dry white wine*	*3 tbsp*
60 g	*crumbled feta cheese*	*2 oz*
2 tbsp	*chopped fresh parsley*	*2 tbsp*
4	*oil-cured black olives, stoned and sliced*	*4*
	freshly ground black pepper	

Preheat the oven to 190°C (375°F or Mark 5). Lightly oil a large baking dish; layer the tomatoes, onions, fennel, garlic and oregano in the bottom. Rinse the fish under cold running water and pat it dry with paper towels. Slice the fish crosswise into pieces about 5 cm (2 inches) wide. Arrange the fish on top of the vegetables and sprinkle it with the wine.

Cover the dish with foil and bake the fish until it is opaque and feels firm to the touch — 15 to 20 minutes. Remove the dish from the oven. Sprinkle the fish with the crumbled feta cheese, parsley, black olives and some pepper. Garnish with some of the reserved fennel tops and serve immediately, spooning the pan juices over each portion.

SUGGESTED ACCOMPANIMENT: *steamed rice.*

Haddock Enchiladas with Chili Sauce

IN MEXICAN COOKING, ENCHILADAS ARE FILLED TORTILLAS SERVED WITH A SAUCE.

Serves 4
Working (and total) time: about 1 hour

Calories **400**
Protein **23g**
Cholesterol **50mg**
Total fat **9g**
Saturated fat **1g**
Sodium **295mg**

350 g	*haddock fillets*	*12 oz*
90 g	*long-grain rice*	*3 oz*
1	*dried hot chili pepper (caution, box opposite), seeded and very finely chopped or ground with a mortar and pestle, or ¼ tsp crushed red pepper flakes*	*1*
¼ tsp	*salt*	*¼ tsp*
	freshly ground black pepper	
2 tbsp	*safflower oil*	*2 tbsp*
1	*garlic clove, finely chopped*	*1*
1	*small onion, finely chopped*	*1*
750 g	*ripe tomatoes, skinned, seeded and coarsely chopped, or 400 g (14 oz) canned tomatoes, drained and coarsely chopped, the juice reserved*	*1½ lb*
12.5 cl	*fish stock (recipe, page 136) or white wine, or substitute the reserved juice of the chopped canned tomatoes*	*4 fl oz*
¼ tsp	*ground cumin*	*¼ tsp*
8	*corn tortillas*	*8*
	Chili sauce	
500 g	*green tomatoes, skinned, seeded and chopped, or tomatillos, husked*	*1 lb*
1	*fresh hot chili pepper, seeded and chopped (caution, box opposite)*	*1*
2 tbsp	*chopped fresh coriander*	*2 tbsp*
1	*small onion, finely chopped*	*1*
	freshly ground black pepper	

Preheat the oven to 190°C (375°F or Mark 5). In a 1 litre (2 pint) fireproof casserole, combine the rice, dried chili pepper, ⅛ teaspoon of the salt and 30 cl (½ pint) of water. Bring to the boil, then cover the casserole tightly and cook in the oven until the rice has absorbed all the liquid and is tender — about 25 minutes.

Meanwhile, make the chili sauce. Put the green tomatoes in a saucepan with 8 cl (3 fl oz) of water and simmer for 5 minutes. (If using tomatillos, simmer them in water to cover for 25 minutes, until soft). Drain, then put them in a food processor or blender. Add the chili pepper, coriander, onion and some black pepper, and blend until a coarse purée results. Set the sauce aside.

Rinse the fillets under cold running water and pat them dry with paper towels. Season the fillets on both sides with the remaining salt and some black pepper.

Heat the oil in a large, heavy frying pan over medium heat. Add the garlic and cook it for 30 seconds, stirring constantly. Add the onion, the fresh tomatoes with the fish stock or wine (or the canned tomatoes with their juice), the cumin and some more black pepper. Bring the mixture to a simmer, then add the fish. Cover the pan and simmer until the fillets can be flaked at their thickest point — about 7 minutes. With a fork, shred the fillets into bite-sized or smaller pieces. Spoon the rice over the fish mixture and stir well to combine.

To assemble the enchiladas, heat a small, heavy frying pan over medium-high heat. Place a tortilla in the pan and warm it for 15 to 30 seconds. Turn the tortilla over and warm it on the second side for 15 to 30 seconds more. Quickly transfer the tortilla to a work surface, and lay the next tortilla in the pan to warm. Spread 6 tablespoons of the fish mixture in a line across the first tortilla, about half way between the middle of the tortilla and the near edge. Working quickly, fold the near edge of the tortilla over the filling and roll it away from you, then place the enchilada, seam side down, in a lightly oiled casserole. Turn the tortilla in the pan and warm it on the second side for 15 to 30 seconds, then fill it while you warm a third tortilla. Warm and fill the remaining tortillas in the same manner and place them snugly side by side in the casserole.

Pour the chili sauce over the enchiladas and warm the casserole in the oven until they are heated through — 7 to 10 minutes. Serve immediately.

EDITOR'S NOTE: *Tomatillos are the more authentic ingredient in Mexico, but green tomatoes make a good substitute.*

Chili Peppers — a Cautionary Note

Both dried and fresh hot chili peppers should be handled with care. Their flesh and seeds contain volatile oils that can make skin tingle and cause eyes to burn. Rubber gloves offer protection — but the cook should still be careful not to touch the face, lips or eyes when working with chilies.

Soaking fresh chili peppers in cold, salted water for an hour will remove some of their fire. If canned chilies are substituted for fresh ones, they should be rinsed in cold water in order to eliminate as much of the brine used to preserve them as possible.

Baked Coley with Tomatoes, Courgettes and Provolone

Serves 4
Working time: about 15 minutes
Total time: about 30 minutes

Calories **215**
Protein **27g**
Cholesterol **90mg**
Total fat **9g**
Saturated fat **3g**
Sodium **360mg**

500 g	*coley fillets (or cod or haddock)*	*1 lb*
¼ tsp	*salt*	*¼ tsp*
	freshly ground black pepper	
1 tbsp	*virgin olive oil*	*1 tbsp*
2 tbsp	*chopped fresh basil, or 1 tbsp dried basil*	*2 tbsp*
2	*garlic cloves, finely chopped*	*2*
750 g	*ripe tomatoes, skinned, seeded and chopped, or 400 g (14 oz) canned whole tomatoes, drained, chopped and drained again*	*1½ lb*
1	*small courgette, sliced diagonally into thin ovals*	*1*
60 g	*provolone cheese, cut into thin, narrow strips*	*2 oz*

Preheat the oven to 200°C (400°F or Mark 6). Rinse the fillets under cold running water and pat them dry with paper towels. Sprinkle ⅛ teaspoon of the salt and some pepper over both sides of the fillets. Spread the oil in the bottom of an ovenproof casserole. Arrange the fillets in the casserole in a single layer.

Strew the basil and garlic over the fish, then cover the fish with the tomatoes. Arrange the courgette slices in a fish-scale pattern down the centre of the dish; sprinkle the remaining salt over them. Cover the dish with a piece of oiled greaseproof paper and bake it for 10 minutes. Remove the greaseproof paper and place the strips of provolone in a diamond pattern around the courgette. Cover the dish again and bake it until the fish feels firm to the touch — 3 to 5 minutes more. Serve immediately.

Hake and Four Peppers

Serves 6
Working (and total) time: about 30 minutes

Calories **210**
Protein **23g**
Cholesterol **60mg**
Total fat **6g**
Saturated fat **1g**
Sodium **275mg**

750 g	*skinned hake fillet*	*1½ lb*
1 tsp	*chili powder*	*1 tsp*
⅛ tsp	*cayenne pepper*	*⅛ tsp*
2 tsp	*dried thyme*	*2 tsp*
2 tbsp	*virgin olive oil*	*2 tbsp*
½ tsp	*salt*	*½ tsp*
3	*sweet green peppers, seeded and deribbed, 1 coarsely chopped, the remaining 2 diced*	*3*
2 or 3	*fresh hot green chili peppers, seeded and chopped (caution, page 45)*	*2 or 3*
2	*onions, chopped*	*2*
3	*garlic cloves, finely chopped*	*3*
2	*bay leaves*	*2*
35 cl	*dry white wine*	*12 fl oz*
1	*sweet red pepper, seeded, deribbed and diced*	*1*

Preheat the oven to 180°C (350°F or Mark 4).

In a small bowl, combine the chili powder, cayenne pepper and 1 teaspoon of the thyme. Rinse the fish under cold running water and pat it dry with paper towels. Slice the fish into six equal pieces; sprinkle the spice mixture evenly over the fish.

Heat the oil in a large, heavy frying pan over medium-high heat. When the oil is hot, add the fish pieces and cook them on the first side for 3 minutes. Turn the pieces over and sprinkle them with ¼ teaspoon of the salt. Cook the fish on the second side for 2 minutes. Transfer the fish to an ovenproof dish and bake them for 5 minutes.

Meanwhile, add the diced green peppers, the green chilies, onions, garlic, bay leaves and the remaining thyme to the frying pan. Cook the mixture, stirring often, for 5 minutes. Stir in the wine, red pepper and remaining salt.

Remove the fish from the oven and pour into the pan any juices that have collected in the bottom of the dish. Return the fish to the oven for 5 minutes to finish baking it. Increase the heat under the pan and cook the pepper mixture until most of the liquid has evaporated — about 5 minutes. Remove the bay leaves.

While the pepper mixture and fish are cooking, purée the coarsely chopped green pepper in a food processor or blender. Stir the purée into the pepper mixture in the pan and cook it for 1 minute more.

Remove the fish from the oven and spoon about half of the vegetables round it. Pass the remaining vegetables in a bowl.

SUGGESTED ACCOMPANIMENT: *steamed new potatoes.*

Curried Grouper

Serves 4
Working time: about 15 minutes
Total time: about 25 minutes

Calories **260**
Protein **25g**
Cholesterol **40mg**
Total fat **8g**
Saturated fat **1g**
Sodium **230mg**

500 g	*grouper fillet (or monkfish)*	*1 lb*
1 tbsp	*curry powder*	*1 tbsp*
2 tbsp	*safflower oil*	*2 tbsp*
3 tbsp	*fresh lime juice*	*3 tbsp*
	freshly ground black pepper	
1	*large red apple, cored and cut into pieces*	*1*
125 g	*chopped onion*	*4 oz*
1 tsp	*fennel seeds, cracked*	*1 tsp*
¼ tsp	*salt*	*¼ tsp*
150 g	*shelled peas, blanched in boiling water for 1 minute*	*5 oz*
	dry white wine	

Rinse the fillet under cold running water and pat it dry with paper towels. Cut the fillet into 2.5 cm (1 inch) pieces.

In a small bowl, combine the curry powder, 1 tablespoon of the oil, the lime juice and some pepper. Put the fish pieces, apple, onion and fennel seeds into a large bowl. Pour the curry mixture over the fish and mix well. Let the fish marinate for 10 minutes.

Pour the remaining oil into a large, heavy frying pan over high heat. When the oil is hot, add the contents of the bowl. Sprinkle in the salt and cook the curry for 3 minutes, stirring constantly. Add the peas and white wine and continue cooking the curry, stirring often, until the fish is firm to the touch — 2 to 3 minutes more. Transfer the curry to a warmed serving dish.

SUGGESTED ACCOMPANIMENTS: *mango chutney; diced cucumbers; unsalted peanuts; steamed rice.*

Grouper with Shiitake Mushroom Sauce

Serves 4
Working (and total) time: about 35 minutes

Calories **210**
Protein **23g**
Cholesterol **40mg**
Total fat **8g**
Saturated fat **1g**
Sodium **400mg**

500 g	*whole grouper fillet (or haddock or monkfish)*	*1 lb*
15 g	*dried shiitake or other Oriental mushrooms, soaked in 17.5 cl (6 fl oz) very hot water for 20 minutes*	*½ oz*
4 tbsp	*dry sherry*	*4 tbsp*
2 tbsp	*low-sodium soy sauce or shoyu*	*2 tbsp*
2 tbsp	*fresh lime juice*	*2 tbsp*
1 tsp	*sugar*	*1 tsp*
1½ tsp	*cornflour*	*1½ tsp*
2 tbsp	*safflower oil*	*2 tbsp*
2	*spring onions, trimmed and thinly sliced*	*2*
1 tbsp	*julienned fresh ginger root*	*1 tbsp*
2	*garlic cloves, thinly sliced*	*2*
½ tsp	*freshly ground black pepper*	*½ tsp*

Remove the mushrooms from their soaking liquid and slice them into thin pieces. Set the mushrooms aside. Pour 4 tablespoons of the soaking liquid into a mixing bowl, being careful to leave any grit from the mushrooms behind. Stir in the sherry, soy sauce, 1 tablespoon of the lime juice and the sugar. Set the mixture aside.

Rinse the fillet under cold running water and pat it dry. Rub the fillet with the remaining lime juice, then rub the cornflour evenly over both sides of the fish.

Heat the oil in a large, heavy frying pan (preferably non-stick) over high heat. When the oil is hot, add the fish and sear it on one side for 2 minutes. Carefully turn the fillet over and sear it on the second side for 2 minutes. Transfer the fish to a plate.

Add the mushrooms, spring onions, ginger, garlic and pepper to the hot pan. Cook the mixture on high for 1 minute, then reduce the heat to low. Pour in the sherry mixture, replace the fillet, and cover the pan. Steam the fish until it is opaque — about 5 minutes. Transfer the fish to a warmed serving platter and spoon the sauce around it.

SUGGESTED ACCOMPANIMENT: *stir-fried red cabbage.*

2 *Chilled to preserve their savour, such rich-fleshed fish as shad and salmon tempt with plump goodness..*

The Virtues of Richness

The recipes that follow feature the so-called fatty or oily fish — all those whose flesh has more than a 5 per cent fat content. Now that such rich-fleshed fish are seen as being healthy, there is more reason than ever to enjoy them. Happily, among them are such popular species as salmon, tuna, mackerel and trout. Thanks to their high concentrations of certain polyunsaturated oils, which amount to close to 15 per cent in several varieties, they appear to be uniquely helpful in lowering the levels of triglycerides in humans. Indeed, the oil in fish may be one of nature's best preventives against heart disease.

Because their natural oils baste them as they cook, rich-fleshed fish respond well to grilling, baking and barbecuing. (Do not let this fool you: they are as easy to overcook, and therefore ruin, as the leaner fish.) The firm flesh of some varieties also makes them prime candidates for sautéing, stir-frying and poaching. What could be easier to prepare — or finer to eat — than lightly sautéed salmon, served with the basil and shallot sauce on page 70?

Rich-fleshed fish have pronounced flavour. They may need citrus juice or wine to tame or mellow it. At the same time, they retain their identity when cooked with garlic, peppers and various other aromatic vegetables. In this section, mackerel is grilled and then set off by a rhubarb-orange sauce. Grey mullet, marinated in a mixture of vinegar, lemon juice and garlic, then grilled under a coat of cracked black pepper, is served with a sauce made with the remaining marinade, fish stock, thyme and a little butter.

The rich-fleshed fish are best caught and savoured when their oil content is highest. For example, salmon is at its most glorious just before it begins its summer spawning runs. For cooks lucky enough to catch their own rich-fleshed fish, or for those who like to buy them whole and cut them up at home, step-by-step instructions for cleaning and filleting the fish appear on pages 128-130.

Stuffed Herrings

Serves 4
Working time: about 45 minutes
Total time: about 1 hour and 25 minutes

Calories **530**
Protein **36g**
Cholesterol **130mg**
Total fat **40g**
Saturated fat **9g**
Sodium **350mg**

4	*herrings (350 g/12 oz each), dressed (pages 128-129)*	*4*
15 g	*unsalted butter*	*½ oz*
1	*onion, finely chopped*	*1*
175 g	*mushrooms, chopped*	*6 oz*
1	*lemon, rind only, finely grated*	*1*
1 tbsp	*lemon juice*	*1 tbsp*
1 tbsp	*chopped parsley*	*1 tbsp*
1 tsp	*fresh thyme leaves*	*1 tsp*
60 g	*fresh white breadcrumbs*	*2 oz*
¼ tsp	*salt*	*¼ tsp*
	freshly ground black pepper	
	Garnish	
	sliced mushrooms	
	parsley	
	lemon wedges	

Preheat the oven to 200°C (400°F or Mark 6).

Wash the herrings thoroughly then pat them dry with paper towels. To remove the bones, take one fish at a time and place it on a work surface belly down. Gently but firmly press along the length of the backbone to flatten the fish. Turn the herring over, and run a thumb under the bones at each side of the backbone to loosen. Lift the bones out in one piece and snip the bone 2.5 cm (1 inch) from the tail.

Melt the butter in a heavy frying pan, add the onion and cook for 4 to 5 minutes until softened but not browned. Add the mushrooms and cook for 3 to 4 minutes until they are softened. Stir in the lemon rind and juice, parsley, thyme and breadcrumbs. Season with the salt and pepper. Lay the herrings flat out, flesh side up. Spread some stuffing over each herring, then roll up from head to tail. Secure them by pressing the small piece of tail bone remaining into the flesh.

Place the herrings in a buttered ovenproof dish, cover with foil and bake until the fish feels firm to the touch — about 35 minutes. Serve hot, garnished with mushrooms, parsley and lemon wedges.

Baked Herrings with Yogurt-Mint Sauce

Serves 4
Working time: about 15 minutes
Total time: about 1 hour

Calories **340**
Protein **35g**
Cholesterol **95mg**
Total fat **18g**
Saturated fat **5g**
Sodium **200mg**

4	*herrings (or mackerel), about 250 g (8 oz) each, dressed (pages 128-129)*	*4*
4 tbsp	*chopped fresh mint*	*4 tbsp*
4	*garlic cloves, finely chopped*	*4*
¼ tsp	*ground cumin*	*¼ tsp*
¼ tsp	*cayenne pepper*	*¼ tsp*
	Yogurt-mint sauce	
2 tbsp	*chopped fresh mint*	*2 tbsp*
¼ litre	*plain low-fat yogurt*	*8 fl oz*
1 tbsp	*virgin olive oil*	*1 tbsp*
3	*garlic cloves, finely chopped*	*3*
¼ tsp	*ground cumin*	*¼ tsp*
¼ tsp	*ground coriander*	*¼ tsp*
¼ tsp	*ground turmeric*	*¼ tsp*
¼ tsp	*ground cardamom (optional)*	*¼ tsp*
	mint sprigs for garnish	

Rinse the herrings under cold running water and pat them dry with paper towels.

In a small bowl, combine the 4 tablespoons of chopped mint, the garlic, cumin and cayenne pepper. Spread one quarter of this mixture inside the cavity of each herring. Cut shallow diagonal slashes at 2.5 cm (1 inch) intervals along the sides of each fish. Lay the fish on their sides in a lightly oiled baking dish. Let the herrings marinate at room temperature for 30 minutes. Preheat the oven to 240°C (475°F or Mark 9).

While the fish is marinating, prepare the sauce. Stir the 2 tablespoons of chopped mint into the yogurt in a bowl, and set it aside. Heat the oil in a small heavy frying pan over medium-high heat, add the garlic and cook it until it is soft — about 2 minutes. Stir in the cumin, coriander, turmeric, and cardamom if you are using it, and cook the mixture for 30 seconds. Add the spice mixture to the minted yogurt and stir well.

Bake the fish until it feels firm to the touch and is opaque throughout — about 12 minutes. Serve it immediately, accompanied by the sauce and garnished with the mint sprigs.

SUGGESTED ACCOMPANIMENT: *steamed carrots.*

Baked Grey Mullet

Serves 4
Working time: about 25 minutes
Total time: about 1 hour and 10 minutes

Calories **280**
Protein **40g**
Cholesterol **100mg**
Total fat **10g**
Saturated fat **4g**
Sodium **230mg**

1	*grey mullet (1.5 to 2 kg/3 to 4 lb)*	1
½ tsp	*salt*	½ tsp
	freshly ground black pepper	
1	*large parsley sprig*	1
1	*large fresh thyme sprig*	1
1	*large fresh rosemary sprig*	1
1	*small lemon, cut into wedges*	1
15 g	*unsalted butter*	½ oz
2	*large onions, thinly sliced*	2
3	*garlic cloves, peeled and sliced*	3
1 tbsp	*virgin olive oil*	1 tbsp
4 tbsp	*dry white wine*	4 tbsp
	lemon slices for garnish	

Preheat the oven to 200°C (400°F or Mark 6). Remove the fins, scales and viscera (but not the head) from the mullet, as demonstrated on pages 128-129. Wash the fish thoroughly under cold running water, then pat it dry with paper towels.

Season the inside of the mullet with a little of the salt and some pepper, and insert the parsley, thyme and rosemary sprigs and the lemon wedges.

Butter a large, shallow baking dish, then place the onion and garlic slices in the bottom of the dish. Set the mullet on top of the onion and garlic, and season with the remaining salt and more pepper. Sprinkle the fish with the olive oil and white wine. Cover the dish with aluminium foil and bake the mullet in the oven until it is firm to the touch — 40 to 45 minutes. Serve hot, garnished with lemon slices.

EDITOR'S NOTE: *If you do not have a large baking dish, the mullet may be cooked wrapped in foil on a large baking sheet.*
SUGGESTED ACCOMPANIMENT: *baked courgettes and tomatoes.*

Grilled Mullet Coated with Cracked Black Pepper

Serves 6
Working time: about 35 minutes
Total time: about 4 hours and 30 minutes

Calories **150**
Protein **21g**
Cholesterol **85mg**
Total fat **5g**
Saturated fat **3g**
Sodium **180mg**

750 g	*grey mullet fillets (or powan), skinned*	*1½ lb*
6 tbsp	*fresh lemon juice*	*6 tbsp*
12.5 cl	*red wine vinegar*	*4 fl oz*
3	*garlic cloves, crushed*	*3*
1½ tbsp	*sugar*	*1½ tbsp*
¼ tsp	*salt*	*¼ tsp*
3 tbsp	*black peppercorns, cracked*	*3 tbsp*
17.5 cl	*fish stock (recipe, page 136) or vegetable stock*	*6 fl oz*
2 tsp	*fresh thyme, or ½ tsp dried thyme*	*2 tsp*
30 g	*cold unsalted butter, cut into small pieces*	*1 oz*
2	*thyme sprigs for garnish*	*2*

In a shallow bowl just large enough to hold the fillets in a single layer, stir together the lemon juice, red wine vinegar, crushed garlic, sugar and salt. Lay the fillets in the liquid, cover the bowl and let the fish marinate in the refrigerator for at least 4 hours; half way through the marinating time, turn the fillets over.

Preheat the grill or, if you are barbecuing, light the charcoal about 40 minutes before cooking time. Remove the fillets from the marinade and pat them dry with paper towels. Sprinkle half of the cracked pepper over the fillets and press the pepper firmly into the flesh with your fingertips. Turn the fillets over and coat them with the remaining black pepper in the same manner.

If you are grilling the fillets, cook them about 10 cm (4 inches) below the heat source for 4 to 5 minutes on each side.

If you are barbecuing the fillets, place them approximately 10 cm (4 inches) above the heat source and cook them on the first side for 6 minutes. Gently turn the fillets over and cook them on the second side until their flesh just flakes — about 6 minutes more.

While the fish is cooking, strain the marinade into a small non-reactive saucepan over medium heat and add the stock and thyme. Cook the mixture until it is reduced to about 12.5 cl (4 fl oz) — approximately 5 minutes. When the fillets are cooked, transfer them to a heated serving platter. Whisk the butter into the sauce, pour the sauce over the fillets, garnish with the thyme sprigs, and serve at once.

SUGGESTED ACCOMPANIMENT: *tomato salad sprinkled with chopped spring onions.*

Spicy Grilled Shad

THE FINE ART OF BONING SHAD FILLETS IS DESCRIBED BELOW. IF YOU PREFER, A RELIABLE FISHMONGER CAN BONE THEM FOR YOU.

Serves 6
Working time: about 30 minutes
Total time: about 1 hour

Calories **250**
Protein **20g**
Cholesterol **90mg**
Total fat **17g**
Saturated fat **6g**
Sodium **60mg**

2	*shad fillets, about 350 g (12 oz) each, (or rainbow trout or sea trout), unskinned*	*2*
2 tbsp	*dry vermouth*	*2 tbsp*
1	*lime, juice only*	*1*
½	*orange, juice only*	*½*
1	*fresh hot green chili pepper, seeded and finely chopped (caution, page 45)*	*1*
1	*garlic clove, finely chopped*	*1*
1 tsp	*fresh thyme, or ¼ tsp dried thyme*	*1 tsp*
⅛ tsp	*ground allspice*	*⅛ tsp*
20 g	*unsalted butter, cut into small cubes*	*¾ oz*

In a small bowl, combine the vermouth, lime juice, orange juice, chili pepper, garlic, thyme and allspice. Set the bowl aside.

Rinse the shad fillets under cold running water and pat them dry with paper towels. To bone the fillets, place one of them skin side down on a work surface. With your fingers, locate the two rows of small bones; each row lies about 2.5 cm (1 inch) on either side of the centre line of the fillet. Using a small, sharp knife, make a long cut on either side of one of the rows; take care not to penetrate the skin. Working from the head end towards the tail, gently pull the bones away in a single strip. Repeat the process to remove the other row of bones; bone the remaining fillet in the same manner.

Lay the fillets in an ovenproof dish and pour the marinade over them. Let the fillets marinate for 15 minutes. Preheat the grill.

Strain and reserve the marinade. Grill the fillets about 7.5 cm (3 inches) below the heat source, basting them every 3 minutes with the marinade, until their flesh is opaque — 10 to 12 minutes. Scatter the cubes of butter over the top; return the fillets to the grill and cook them a few seconds longer to melt the butter. Serve immediately.

SUGGESTED ACCOMPANIMENT: *salad of tropical fruits.*

Skewered Sardines with Watercress Sauce

Serves 4
Working time: about 50 minutes
Total time: about 1 hour and 50 minutes

Calories **420**
Protein **35g**
Cholesterol **90mg**
Total fat **25g**
Saturated fat **7g**
Sodium **230mg**

8	*sardines weighing 125 g (4 oz) each, or 1 kg (2 lb) small sardines*	8
½ tsp	*cayenne pepper*	½ tsp
24	*black peppercorns, crushed*	24
1 tbsp	*virgin olive oil*	1 tbsp
½ tsp	*salt*	½ tsp
1	*lime, rind only, finely grated*	1
	watercress sprigs for garnish	
	lemon wedges (optional)	
	Watercress sauce	
30 cl	*fish stock (recipe, page 136)*	½ pint
125 g	*watercress, trimmed and washed*	4 oz
15 g	*unsalted butter*	½ oz
15 g	*flour*	½ oz
1 tbsp	*double cream*	1 tbsp

Remove the fins, scales and viscera, but not the heads, from the sardines, as demonstrated on pages 128-129. Wash the fish under cold running water, then drain them dry on paper towels.

Put the cayenne pepper, peppercorns, oil, salt and grated lime rind in a large, shallow dish and mix them together. Place the sardines in the marinade, turning them until evenly coated. Cover and marinate for 1 hour.

To make the sauce, pour the fish stock into a small saucepan and bring to the boil. Add the watercress and cook gently for 10 minutes, until softened, then purée in a food processor or blender for 1 minute.

Melt the butter in the pan, stir in the flour, then the puréed watercress. Bring to the boil, stirring all the time. Reduce the heat and simmer the sauce for 10 to 15 minutes.

Meanwhile, remove the sardines from the marinade and thread them on to wooden or metal skewers. Cook under a hot grill for 4 to 5 minutes, turning them once during cooking.

Stir the cream into the sauce then pour into a jug. Serve the sardines garnished with watercress and, if liked, lemon wedges. Hand the sauce separately.

Poached Turbot in Orange-Lemon Sauce

Serves 4
Working (and total) time: about 30 minutes

Calories **285**
Protein **16g**
Cholesterol **70mg**
Total fat **18g**
Saturated fat **6g**
Sodium **230mg**

500 g	*turbot fillets (or flounder, halibut or sole)*	*1 lb*
17.5 cl	*fish stock (recipe, page 136)*	*6 fl oz*
17.5 cl	*dry white wine*	*6 fl oz*
15 cl	*fresh orange juice*	*¼ pint*
1 tbsp	*fresh lemon juice*	*1 tbsp*
2	*shallots, finely chopped*	*2*
1 tbsp	*fresh thyme, or 1 tsp dried thyme*	*1 tbsp*
	freshly ground black pepper	
30 g	*unsalted butter*	*1 oz*
1	*large lettuce (about 150 g/5 oz), cored and washed*	*1*
¼ tsp	*salt*	*¼ tsp*

To prepare the poaching liquid, combine the fish stock, white wine, orange juice, lemon juice, half of the chopped shallots, half of the thyme and some black pepper in a large, non-reactive sauté pan. Bring the liquid to the boil, then reduce the heat to medium low. Simmer the liquid for 10 minutes.

Rinse the fillets under cold running water and pat them dry with paper towels. Slice each fillet diagonally in half to form one thick piece and one thin piece. Place the thicker fillets in the simmering liquid and poach them gently for 1 minute. Add the thinner fillets and continue poaching the fish until it is opaque and feels firm to the touch — 3 to 4 minutes. Transfer the fish to a plate and keep it warm.

Raise the heat to medium and simmer the poaching liquid until it is reduced to about 12.5 cl (4 fl oz). Strain the sauce through a sieve into a small pan and set it aside.

Melt 15 g (½ oz) of the butter in the same pan over medium heat. Add the remaining shallots and thyme, and cook them for 1 minute, stirring. Add the lettuce leaves, ⅛ teaspoon of the salt and some pepper. Cook the lettuce, stirring, until it has wilted — approximately 2 minutes. Place the lettuce on a warmed serving plate.

Reheat the sauce; stir in the remaining salt and whisk in the remaining butter. Put the fish pieces on the wilted lettuce, pour the sauce over the fish and serve immediately.

SUGGESTED ACCOMPANIMENT: *steamed courgettes with diced sweet red pepper.*

Turbot Salad

Serves 4 as a starter
Working time: about 30 minutes
Total time: about 2 hours

Calories **220**
Protein **30g**
Cholesterol **95mg**
Total fat **9g**
Saturated fat **1g**
Sodium **320mg**

1 kg	*turbot, cleaned*	*2 lb*
60 cl	*court-bouillon (recipe, page 136)*	*1 pint*
2 tbsp	*virgin olive oil*	*2 tbsp*
1	*lemon, rind only, finely grated*	*1*
2 tbsp	*lemon juice*	*2 tbsp*
½ tsp	*ground cardamom*	*½ tsp*
1 tbsp	*chopped mixed herbs (parsley, marjoram and chives)*	*1 tbsp*
½ tsp	*salt*	*½ tsp*
	freshly ground black pepper	
2 tbsp	*chopped spring onions*	*2 tbsp*
2	*kiwi fruit, peeled and sliced*	*2*
350 g	*tomatoes, sliced*	*12 oz*
1 tbsp	*finely shredded basil leaves*	*1 tbsp*
	watercress sprigs for garnish	

Rinse the turbot well under cold running water, removing any remaining viscera.

Pour the court-bouillon into a wide shallow saucepan. Place the turbot in the court-bouillon, cover the saucepan and cook for 10 minutes, or until the flesh flakes easily. Leave the turbot to cool in the court-bouillon — about 1½ hours.

Take the turbot out of the court-bouillon and skin it. Carefully remove the flesh from the bones, break the flesh into large flakes and set aside.

Place the olive oil, grated lemon rind, lemon juice, cardamom, mixed herbs, ¼ teaspoon of the salt and some pepper in a mixing bowl and blend them well together. Add the spring onions, the flaked turbot and sliced kiwi fruit and mix gently.

Arrange the tomato slices neatly on a large serving plate or on individual plates. Season the tomatoes with the rest of the salt and some pepper, then sprinkle them with the basil. Spoon the turbot salad on to the tomatoes, garnish with the watercress sprigs and serve.

EDITOR'S NOTE: *The court-bouillon in which the turbot has been cooked makes an excellent fish stock. Strain and freeze it, or reserve it for later use.*

Baked Powan with Garlic and Glazed Carrots

Serves 4
Working time: about 15 minutes
Total time: about 1 hour

Calories **265**
Protein **23g**
Cholesterol **55mg**
Total fat **14g**
Saturated fat **2g**
Sodium **270mg**

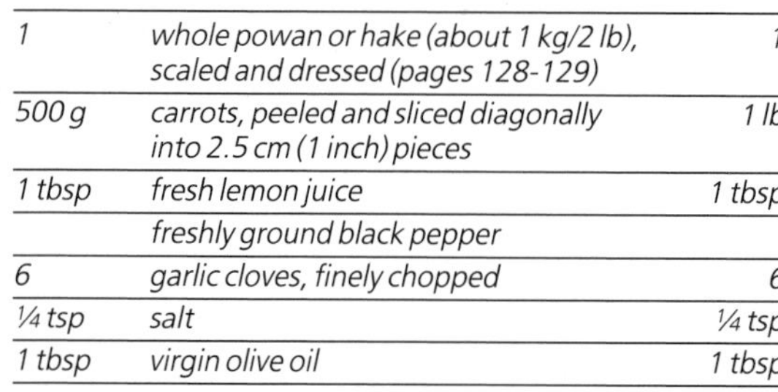

1	*whole powan or hake (about 1 kg/2 lb), scaled and dressed (pages 128-129)*	*1*
500 g	*carrots, peeled and sliced diagonally into 2.5 cm (1 inch) pieces*	*1 lb*
1 tbsp	*fresh lemon juice*	*1 tbsp*
	freshly ground black pepper	
6	*garlic cloves, finely chopped*	*6*
¼ tsp	*salt*	*¼ tsp*
1 tbsp	*virgin olive oil*	*1 tbsp*

Preheat the oven to 200°C (400°F or Mark 6). Put the carrots in a baking dish large enough to take the fish. Add the lemon juice, a generous grinding of pepper and a third of the chopped garlic. Pour 17.5 cl (6 fl oz) of water into the dish and toss the ingredients well.

Sprinkle the fish inside and out with the salt and some pepper, and rub the remaining garlic all over it. Push the carrots to the sides of the dish and lay the fish on the bottom. Dribble the oil over the fish. Bake, stirring the carrots every 15 minutes, until the fish is golden and the carrots are tender — about 45 minutes.

SUGGESTED ACCOMPANIMENT: *Brussels sprouts.*

Carp in Red Wine

Serves 6
Working time: about 40 minutes
Total time: about 1 hour and 40 minutes

Calories **335**
Protein **18g**
Cholesterol **70mg**
Total fat **13g**
Saturated fat **3g**
Sodium **160mg**

1	*whole carp or salmon (about 2 kg/4½ lb), dressed (pages 128-129) and cut into 2.5 cm (1 inch) thick steaks*	*1*
250 g	*pearl onions*	*8 oz*
¾ litre	*red wine*	*1¼ pints*
¾ litre	*fish stock (recipe, page 136)*	*1¼ pints*
3	*whole cloves*	*3*
1	*small cinnamon stick*	*1*
12	*black peppercorns*	*12*
¼ tsp	*salt*	*¼ tsp*
1	*bay leaf*	*1*
1 tbsp	*safflower oil*	*1 tbsp*
250 g	*mushrooms, wiped clean, trimmed and thickly sliced*	*8 oz*
1 tsp	*sugar*	*1 tsp*
4 tbsp	*sultanas*	*4 tbsp*
15 g	*cold unsalted butter, cut into small pieces*	*½ oz*
6	*chervil or parsley sprigs*	*6*

Cut off the root ends of the onions. Put them in a bowl and pour in enough boiling water to cover them. When the water has cooled — about 15 minutes — remove the onions and squeeze them out of their skins. Set them aside.

In a large, heavy sauté pan, combine the wine, stock, cloves, cinnamon, peppercorns, salt and bay leaf. Bring the liquid to the boil, then reduce the heat to medium and simmer the mixture for 10 minutes.

Rinse the carp steaks under cold running water. Lay the steaks in the pan and poach them, uncovered, until the flesh is opaque and feels firm to the touch —about 10 minutes. Remove the steaks; cover them with aluminium foil and keep them warm.

Return the poaching liquid to the boil and cook it until it is reduced to ½ litre (16 fl oz) — about 15 minutes.

Meanwhile, prepare the mushrooms and onions. Pour the oil into another large, heavy pan over medium-high heat. When the oil is hot, add the mushrooms and sauté them until tender and golden — about 4 minutes. Use a slotted spoon to transfer the mushrooms to a bowl, and set them aside. Add the onions, sugar and ¼ litre (8 fl oz) of water to the pan. Cook the mixture until the water has evaporated and the onions are coated with a golden glaze — about 7 minutes. Using the slotted spoon, transfer the onions to the bowl with the mushrooms.

Strain the reduced stock into the pan you used to cook the onions. Add the sultanas and bring the liquid to the boil. Simmer the mixture, scraping and stirring to dissolve the caramelized juices, until the liquid is reduced to about ¼ litre (8 fl oz) — about 5 minutes. Reduce the heat to low and whisk in the butter. Add the reserved mushrooms and onions and reheat them, then pour the sauce over the steaks. Garnish with the sprigs of chervil or parsley, and serve immediately.

SUGGESTED ACCOMPANIMENT: *yellow squash or courgettes.*

Carp with Paprika and Dill Cucumber Sauce

Serves 4
Working time: about 40 minutes
Total time: about 1 hour and 30 minutes

Calories **400**
Protein **45g**
Cholesterol **170mg**
Total fat **22g**
Saturated fat **6g**
Sodium **265mg**

1	*carp (about 1.5 kg/3 lb)*	*1*
½ tsp	*salt*	*½ tsp*
	freshly ground black pepper	
1 tbsp	*lemon juice*	*1 tbsp*
1	*small bunch fresh dill*	*1*
1	*small bunch fresh parsley*	*1*
15 g	*butter*	*½ oz*
1 tbsp	*olive oil*	*1 tbsp*
1	*large onion, finely chopped*	*1*
1	*garlic clove, crushed*	*1*
1 tbsp	*paprika*	*1 tbsp*
12.5 cl	*fish stock (recipe, page 136)*	*4 fl oz*
15 g	*flour*	*½ oz*
12.5 cl	*soured cream*	*4 fl oz*
2	*large pickled dill cucumbers, chopped*	*2*
	Garnish	
	lemon slices	
	sliced pickled dill cucumber	
	chopped parsley and dill	

Preheat the oven to 200°C (400°F or Mark 6).

Remove the fins, scales and viscera (but not the head) from the carp, as demonstrated on pages 128-129. Wash the carp thoroughly under cold running water then pat it dry with paper towels.

Season the inside of the carp with half the salt, some pepper and the lemon juice. Place the dill and parsley inside the carp then set aside.

Heat the butter and oil in a frying pan, add the onion and cook over a low heat for 5 to 6 minutes until the onion is softened but not browned. Stir the garlic and paprika into the onion, then pour in 4 tablespoons of the fish stock and bring to the boil.

Pour the onion mixture into a shallow ovenproof dish and place the carp on top. Cover the dish with foil and cook the carp in the oven until it feels firm to the touch — about 45 to 50 minutes.

With the aid of a large fish slice, carefully lift the carp from the baking dish on to a hot serving dish. Cover and keep warm while making the sauce.

Unless the baking dish is fireproof, transfer the onion and cooking juices to a saucepan, then stir in the flour and the remaining fish stock. Bring the sauce to the boil, stirring all the time. Stir in the soured cream, pickled cucumbers and remaining salt. Reduce the heat to low and simmer for 3 to 4 minutes. Pour into a hot serving bowl or jug.

Garnish with lemon, pickled cucumber and dill. Serve immediately, accompanied by the sauce.

Spiced Carp with Almonds and Raisins

Serves 4
Working time: about 25 minutes
Total time: about 50 minutes

Calories **300**
Protein **25g**
Cholesterol **170mg**
Total fat **17g**
Saturated fat **7g**
Sodium **275mg**

1.5 kg	*carp, dressed (page 128-129) and cut into steaks, about 4 cm (1½ inches) thick*	*3 lb*
½ tsp	*salt*	*½ tsp*
	freshly ground black pepper	
½ tbsp	*olive oil*	*½ tbsp*
60 g	*almonds, blanched and halved*	*2 oz*
15 g	*unsalted butter*	*½ oz*
60 g	*raisins*	*2 oz*
¼ tsp	*ground cumin*	*¼ tsp*
¼ tsp	*ground allspice*	*¼ tsp*
¼ tsp	*ground mace*	*¼ tsp*
¼ tsp	*ground cinnamon*	*¼ tsp*
	Garnish	
	orange wedges	
	parsley	

Preheat the oven to 200°C (400°F or Mark 6).

Lay a piece of aluminium foil on a baking sheet, place the carp steaks side by side on the foil and season with the salt and some pepper.

Heat the oil in a heavy frying pan, add the almonds and fry them gently until lightly browned. Add the butter to the pan and stir in the raisins and spices. Heat for 1 minute, then pour over the carp steaks. Fold the foil to enclose the carp completely and bake in the oven for 25 to 30 minutes, until the flesh is opaque and feels firm to the touch.

Arrange the steaks on a hot serving dish and garnish with orange wedges and parsley. Serve immediately.

Salmon-Stuffed Tuna in Lettuce Leaves

Serves 6
Working time: about 30 minutes
Total time: about 40 minutes

Calories **255**
Protein **35g**
Cholesterol **50mg**
Total fat **10g**
Saturated fat **2g**
Sodium **165mg**

1 kg	*fresh tuna (or swordfish), trimmed and cut into 6 small steaks*	*2 lb*
12	*large round lettuce leaves (or spinach leaves)*	*12*
2	*paper-thin slices smoked salmon, each slice cut into three strips*	*2*
	freshly ground black pepper	
1	*shallot, finely chopped*	*1*
55 cl	*fish stock (recipe, page 136)*	*18 fl oz*
3	*sticks celery, julienned*	*3*
2	*carrots, peeled and julienned*	*2*
1	*large leek, trimmed, washed thoroughly remove all grit, and julienned*	*1*

Blanch the lettuce leaves in a large pan of boiling water for 10 seconds. Refresh them under cold running water. Carefully spread out the leaves — they tear easily — on a cloth. Preheat the oven to 200°C (400°F or Mark 6).

Lightly oil a baking dish large enough to hold the fish steaks in a single layer. With a sharp knife, cut a pocket in the side of one of the steaks. Insert a salmon strip in the pocket, sprinkle the steak with some pepper, and wrap it in two lettuce leaves. Set the wrapped steak in the baking dish. Repeat the process to stuff and wrap the other steaks. Scatter the shallot over the steaks. Bring the stock to the boil and pour ½ litre (16 fl oz) of it over the fish. Cover the dish with aluminium foil, its shiny side down.

Put the fish in the oven; immediately reduce the heat to 180°C (350°F or Mark 4), and bake the fish for 15 minutes.

About 5 minutes before the fish finishes baking, put the celery, carrots and leek in a saucepan. Pour in the remaining stock and turn the heat to medium high. Cover the pan and steam the vegetables until they are tender — 3 to 5 minutes.

Remove the dish from the oven; spoon a little of the fish-cooking liquid into the saucepan with the vegetables, then transfer the vegetables to a warmed serving platter. Carefully transfer the fish to the platter with a fish slice and serve immediately.

SUGGESTED ACCOMPANIMENT: *crusty bread.*

Marinated Fresh Tuna with Peppers

Serves 6 as a first course
Working time: about 30 minutes
Total time: about 2 hours and 30 minutes

Calories **145**
Protein **15g**
Cholesterol **25mg**
Total fat **9g**
Saturated fat **2g**
Sodium **75mg**

350 g	*fresh tuna*	*12 oz*
2 tbsp	*finely chopped red onion*	*2 tbsp*
4 tbsp	*coarsely chopped fresh basil*	*4 tbsp*
2 tbsp	*virgin olive oil*	*2 tbsp*
1 tbsp	*fresh lemon juice*	*1 tbsp*
⅛ tsp	*salt*	*⅛ tsp*
	freshly ground black pepper	
1	*sweet red pepper*	*1*
1	*sweet green pepper*	*1*
1	*sweet yellow pepper*	*1*

Rinse the tuna under cold running water and pat it dry with paper towels. Trim off and discard any dark red meat from the tuna. Cut the tuna into slices about 9 mm (⅜ inch) thick. If any slice is too thick, pound it with the heel of your hand to flatten it. Cut the slices into strips about 1 cm (½ inch) wide and 5 cm (2 inches) long.

Place the tuna strips in a shallow dish with the onion and chopped basil. In a small bowl, whisk together the oil, lemon juice, salt and pepper; pour this mixture over the tuna. With a rubber spatula, toss the tuna very gently until the strips are thoroughly coated. Cover the dish and refrigerate it for 2 hours, turning the tuna strips occasionally.

Preheat the grill. Grill the peppers about 7.5 cm (3 inches) below the heat source, turning them with tongs as they blister, until their skins are blackened all over — approximately 15 minutes. Put the peppers in a large bowl and cover it tightly with plastic film (the trapped steam will loosen their skins). When the peppers are cool enough to handle, peel, seed and derib them. Quarter each pepper lengthwise.

To serve, arrange the marinated tuna strips and the roasted peppers on a platter.

SUGGESTED ACCOMPANIMENT: *French bread.*

EDITOR'S NOTE: *Because the tuna in this recipe is not cooked, only the freshest possible fish should be used.*

Grilled Tuna with White Beans and Red Onions

THE CLASSIC ITALIAN COMBINATION OF TUNA AND BEANS IS ENLIVENED HERE BY THE ADDITION OF PICKLED RED ONIONS.

Serves 6
Working time: about 20 minutes
Total time: about 1 day

Calories **330**
Protein **27g**
Cholesterol **30mg**
Total fat **13g**
Saturated fat **2g**
Sodium **230mg**

500 g	*fresh tuna (or swordfish)*	*1 lb*
180 g	*dried white haricot beans, soaked for at least 8 hours in water*	*6 oz*
2	*garlic cloves*	*2*
1	*strip of lemon rind*	*1*
½ tsp	*salt*	*½ tsp*
2	*large red onions, thinly sliced*	*2*
12.5 cl	*red wine vinegar*	*4 fl oz*
1 tsp	*brown sugar*	*1 tsp*
2	*lemons, juice only*	*2*
3 tbsp	*virgin olive oil*	*3 tbsp*
1½ tsp	*fresh thyme, or ½ tsp dried thyme*	*1½ tsp*
	freshly ground black pepper	
1 tsp	*fresh rosemary, or ¼ tsp dried rosemary*	*1 tsp*
	basil leaves for garnish	

Drain the beans and put them in a saucepan with the garlic and lemon rind. Pour in enough cold water to cover the beans by about 2.5 cm (1 inch). Boil the beans for 10 minutes, then reduce the heat to medium and cook them for 30 minutes. Stir in ¼ teaspoon of the salt and continue cooking the beans until they are tender — 15 to 30 minutes more.

While the beans are cooking, put the onions, vinegar and sugar in a small, non-reactive saucepan over medium-low heat. Simmer the onions, stirring them often, for 10 minutes. Transfer the onions to a small bowl and let them cool slightly, then refrigerate them.

In a mixing bowl, whisk together the lemon juice, 2 tablespoons of the oil, the remaining salt, half of the thyme and a generous grinding of pepper. When the beans are tender, drain them, and discard the lemon rind and garlic cloves. Add the beans to the mixing bowl and stir well.

Preheat the grill. Rinse the tuna under cold running water and pat it dry with paper towels. Trim away any very dark red meat from the tuna. Cut the tuna into 2.5 cm (1 inch) cubes and put the cubes in a fireproof baking dish. Add the remaining oil, the remaining thyme, the rosemary and some pepper, and toss well to coat the tuna. Grill the tuna on the first side for 2 minutes. Turn the pieces over and grill them, watching that they do not overcook, until they are opaque — 1 or 2 minutes more.

Transfer the beans to a serving dish; arrange the tuna cubes on top of the beans and the pickled onions alongside. Garnish the dish with the basil leaves. Serve warm or cold.

SUGGESTED ACCOMPANIMENT: *steamed artichoke hearts.*

Grilled Eel in Ginger-Sherry Sauce on Rice Fingers

Serves 4 as a first course
Working time: about 30 minutes
Total time: about 40 minutes

Calories **420**
Protein **20g**
Cholesterol **95mg**
Total fat **14g**
Saturated fat **3g**
Sodium **370mg**

500 g	*eel*	*1 lb*
1 tsp	*rice vinegar*	*1 tsp*
200 g	*glutinous rice, preferably sushi rice*	*7 oz*
1 tsp	*wasabi (Japanese horseradish powder), mixed with enough water to form a paste*	*1 tsp*
	Ginger-sherry sauce	
4 tbsp	*dry sherry*	*4 tbsp*
2 tbsp	*low-sodium soy sauce or shoyu*	*2 tbsp*
1 tbsp	*finely chopped fresh ginger root*	*1 tbsp*
1 tbsp	*sugar*	*1 tbsp*
1 tbsp	*honey*	*1 tbsp*
⅛ tsp	*cayenne pepper*	*⅛ tsp*

In a saucepan, bring ½ litre (16 fl oz) of water and the vinegar to the boil. Add the rice, tightly cover the pan and reduce the heat to medium low. Cook the rice, stirring occasionally, until all the liquid has been absorbed — about 20 minutes. Set the rice aside to cool.

While the rice is cooking, fillet the eel. Place it on its belly on a cutting board. Cut the head off behind the gills and discard it. Holding a small, sharp knife parallel to the eel, cut along one side of the dorsal fin, following the contour of the backbone along the length of the eel until the fillet is freed. Repeat the process on the other side of the fin to free the second fillet. Cut away any viscera clinging to the fillets. Rinse the fillets under cold running water and cut each in half diagonally.

Pour enough water into a large pan to fill it 1 cm (½ inch) deep. Put a bamboo steamer basket in the water. (Alternatively, put a heatproof cup in the centre of the pan and lay a heatproof plate on top of it.) Place the eel fillets in the steamer basket or on the plate, and bring the water to the boil. Reduce the heat to low, tightly cover the pan and steam the fillets for 7 minutes.

While the fillets are steaming, make the sauce. Combine the sherry, soy sauce, ginger, sugar, honey and cayenne pepper in a small saucepan. Bring the sauce to the boil, then reduce the heat to low. Simmer the sauce until it thickens and is reduced by half — 7 to 10 minutes. Preheat the grill.

Brush some of the sauce on both sides of the fillets and let them stand for 5 minutes. Brush more sauce on the fillets and grill them 7.5 cm (3 inches) below the heat source until they are crisp — 2 to 4 minutes. Carefully turn the fillets over, then brush on more sauce and grill them on the second side until they are crisp — 2 to 3 minutes.

While the eel is cooking, form the cooled rice into 16 ▶

cakes (the Japanese call them "fingers"); each should be about 5 cm (2 inches) long, 2 cm (¾ inch) wide and 2 cm (¾ inch) thick. Arrange the rice fingers on a serving platter or individual plates.

Cut the fillets diagonally into 16 pieces. Set a piece of eel on top of each rice cake; brush the eel pieces with the remaining sauce and serve them with the wasabi.

EDITOR'S NOTE: *Sushi rice, a glutinous rice whose grains cohere well when cooked, is available at Japanese food shops.*

Eel with Spinach and Leeks

Serves 6
Working time: about 20 minutes
Total time: about 40 minutes

Calories **370**
Protein **25g**
Cholesterol **125mg**
Total fat **21g**
Saturated fat **4g**
Sodium **130mg**

1 kg	*eel, skinned, cleaned and cut into 5 cm (2 inch) pieces*	*2 lb*
1 tbsp	*safflower oil*	*1 tbsp*
500 g	*leeks, trimmed, split, washed thoroughly to remove any grit, and sliced*	*1 lb*
2	*garlic cloves, finely chopped*	*2*
1½ tsp	*fresh thyme, or ½ tsp dried thyme*	*1½ tsp*
2 tbsp	*chopped fresh mint*	*2 tbsp*
¼ litre	*dry white wine*	*8 fl oz*
½ litre	*fish stock (recipe, page 136) or unsalted chicken stock*	*16 fl oz*
1 kg	*spinach, washed, stemmed and coarsely chopped*	*2 lb*
2 tbsp	*chopped fresh parsley*	*2 tbsp*

Heat the oil in a large, heavy frying pan over medium heat. Add the leeks, garlic, thyme and 1 tablespoon of the mint. Sauté the mixture for 2 minutes. Pour in the wine, cover the pan, and reduce the heat to medium low; cook the mixture until the leeks are tender — about 10 minutes.

Pour the stock into the pan and bring the liquid to the boil. Add the eel, reduce the heat to maintain a simmer, and cover the pan. Cook until the eel is opaque and feels firm to the touch — about 10 minutes.

About 5 minutes before the eel is done, put the spinach, with only the water that clings to it from washing, in a deep pan. Set the pan over medium-high heat, cover it tightly, and steam the spinach until it is wilted — about 3 minutes. With a slotted spoon, transfer the spinach to a heated serving dish. Arrange the eel pieces on top of the spinach.

Add the remaining mint and the parsley to the eel-cooking liquid. Boil the liquid until it is reduced to ½ litre (16 fl oz) — about 3 minutes. Pour the sauce over the eel and serve immediately.

SUGGESTED ACCOMPANIMENT: *steamed potatoes or rice.*

Sautéed Mackerel with Toasted Hazelnuts

Serves 4
Working (and total) time: about 35 minutes

Calories **440**
Protein **26g**
Cholesterol **120mg**
Total fat **34g**
Saturated fat **9g**
Sodium **320mg**

500 g	*large mackerel fillets*	*1 lb*
45 g	*shelled hazelnuts*	*1½ oz*
2 tbsp	*plain flour*	*2 tbsp*
1 tbsp	*safflower oil*	*1 tbsp*
¼ tsp	*salt*	*¼ tsp*
	freshly ground black pepper	
15 g	*unsalted butter*	*½ oz*
2	*spring onions, trimmed and thinly sliced*	*2*
2	*garlic cloves, finely chopped*	*2*
4 tbsp	*balsamic vinegar, or 3 tbsp red wine vinegar mixed with 1 tsp honey*	*4 tbsp*
1 tbsp	*fresh lime or lemon juice*	*1 tbsp*
1	*tomato, cored and cut into thin strips*	*1*
4 tbsp	*chopped fresh basil or flat-leaf parsley*	*4 tbsp*

Preheat the oven to 180°C (350°F or Mark 4). Spread the hazelnuts in a single layer in a baking tin and toast them in the oven for 10 minutes. Rub the hazelnuts with a tea towel to remove most of their papery skin. Coarsely chop the nuts and set them aside.

Rinse the fillets under cold running water and pat them dry with paper towels. Cut the fillets into a total of four serving pieces and dust them with flour; pat off any excess. Heat the oil in a large, heavy frying pan over medium-high heat. Add the fillets and sauté them on one side for 4 minutes. Turn them over and sprinkle them with the salt and some pepper. Cook the fish on the second side until it feels firm to the touch — 3 to 4 minutes. Transfer the fillets to a serving platter and keep them warm.

Melt the butter in the frying pan. Add the hazelnuts and sauté them for 2 minutes. Stir in the spring onions, garlic, vinegar and citrus juice. Cook the mixture for 1 minute, stirring all the while. Add the tomato, the basil or parsley, and some pepper. Cook the mixture for 1 minute more, stirring constantly, then spread it evenly over the fish. Serve immediately.

SUGGESTED ACCOMPANIMENT: *baked sweet potatoes.*

Salmon with Fresh Basil Sauce

Serves 4
Working time: about 15 minutes
Total time: about 30 minutes

Calories **285**
Protein **24g**
Cholesterol **60mg**
Total fat **18g**
Saturated fat **6g**
Sodium **190mg**

500 g	*salmon fillets, skinned (page 130)*	*1 lb*
1 tbsp	*safflower oil*	*1 tbsp*
¼ tsp	*salt*	*¼ tsp*
	freshly ground black pepper	
1½ tbsp	*fresh lemon juice*	*1½ tbsp*
2	*shallots, thinly sliced*	*2*
1	*garlic clove, finely chopped*	*1*
125 g	*basil leaves*	*4 oz*
4 tbsp	*fish stock (recipe, page 136) or dry white wine*	*4 tbsp*
4 tbsp	*double cream*	*4 tbsp*

Rinse the fillets under cold running water and pat them dry with paper towels. Cut the fish diagonally across the grain into slices about 2.5 cm (1 inch) thick.

Pour the oil into a large, heavy frying pan over high heat. When the oil is hot, add the fish pieces and cook them on the first side for 3 minutes. Carefully turn the pieces over and sprinkle them with ⅛ teaspoon of the salt, a generous grinding of pepper and the lemon juice. Cook them on the second side until they are barely done — about 3 minutes more. Remove the pan from the heat.

Transfer the fish to a warmed serving platter and cover the platter with aluminium foil. Return the pan to the stove over medium heat. Add the shallots and garlic and cook them, stirring constantly, for 30 seconds. Add the basil and the stock or wine, and simmer the mixture for 1 minute. Stir in the cream, the remaining salt and some more pepper, and continue simmering the sauce until it thickens slightly — about 2 minutes. Pour the sauce over the fish and serve immediately.

SUGGESTED ACCOMPANIMENT: *grilled sweet red peppers.*

Pickled Salmon with Red Potatoes

Serves 6 as a first course
Working time: about 25 minutes
Total time: 24 hours

Calories **250**
Protein **24g**
Cholesterol **40mg**
Total fat **11g**
Saturated fat **2g**
Sodium **115mg**

750 g	*fresh salmon fillets, skinned (page 130)*	*1½ lb*
30 g	*fresh dill sprigs*	*1 oz*
2 tbsp	*virgin olive oil*	*2 tbsp*
30 cl	*red wine vinegar or white wine vinegar*	*½ pint*
1	*lemon, juice only*	*1*
1	*orange, juice only*	*1*
1	*bunch spring onions, trimmed and sliced diagonally into 1 cm (½ inch) pieces*	*1*
1 tbsp	*mustard seeds*	*1 tbsp*
1 tsp	*black peppercorns, cracked*	*1 tsp*
3	*bay leaves*	*3*
½ tsp	*salt*	*½ tsp*
1 tsp	*whole cloves*	*1 tsp*
500 g	*red potatoes, skins left on*	*1 lb*

Rinse the fillets under cold running water and pat them dry with paper towels. Cut the fish into chunks about 2 cm (¾ inch) thick.

In a large glass bowl, combine the salmon chunks, three quarters of the dill sprigs and the oil. Put the vinegar, lemon juice, orange juice, spring onions, mustard seeds, peppercorns, bay leaves, salt and cloves in a large, non-reactive saucepan. Bring the mixture to the boil, then pour it over the salmon chunks. Gently stir the marinade and salmon to coat the pieces. Allow the marinade to cool, then cover the bowl and refrigerate it for at least 24 hours.

At the end of the marinating time, strain 17.5 cl (6 fl oz) of the marinade into a second glass bowl. Add the remaining dill sprigs to the strained marinade. Cut the potatoes into 2.5 cm (1 inch) pieces and place them in a steamer. Fill a saucepan about 2.5 cm (1 inch) deep with water. Put the steamer in the saucepan, cover the pan and bring the water to a simmer. Steam the potatoes until they are soft — 10 to 15 minutes. Immediately transfer the potatoes to the strained marinade; stir gently to coat the potatoes.

Serve the hot potatoes at once with the cold salmon.

SUGGESTED ACCOMPANIMENT: *dark rye or wholemeal bread.*

Whole Poached Salmon

Serves 8
Working (and total) time: about 30 minutes

Calories **280**
Protein **28g**
Cholesterol **110mg**
Total fat **17g**
Saturated fat **4g**
Sodium **90mg**

1	*whole salmon (about 2 kg/4 lb), gutted (pages 128-129)*	*1*
4 litres	*court-bouillon (recipe, page 136)*	*7 pints*
	Garnish	
125 g	*spinach, washed, stemmed and thinly sliced*	*4 oz*
250 g	*daikon radish, peeled and julienned*	*8 oz*
1	*red plum, stoned and sliced*	*1*

Pour the court-bouillon into a fish kettle or pan large enough to accommodate the salmon.

Wash the salmon inside and out under cold running water. Wrap the salmon in a double thickness of muslin that is about 25 cm (10 inches) longer than the fish. Knot each end of the muslin and secure it by tying string round the fish in two or three places.

Holding the knotted ends of the cloth, gently lower the fish into the court-bouillon. Bring the liquid to a simmer over medium heat. Cover the pan, reduce the heat to low, and cook the salmon for 8 minutes per 2.5 cm (1 inch) of thickness (measured at its thickest point).

Let the fish cool in the court-bouillon, then carefully transfer it to a work surface. Cut away the strings, untie the knots, and unwrap the muslin, leaving the fish on the cloth. Cut out all but the pectoral fins of the fish. Make a long cut down the back and down the belly of the salmon. Cut through the skin at the base of the tail. Then, working from the base of the tail towards the head, gently pull off the skin in strips.

Carefully transfer the fish to a long platter, placing it skinned side down. Make another cut at the base of the tail and remove the skin from the second side.

Combine the sliced spinach and julienned radish and arrange them round the salmon. Garnish with the plum slices. Serve the salmon warm or cold, accompanied by any number of the sauces that follow.

Each of the sauce recipes below yields one third of the amount of sauce necessary to accompany the salmon. If you decide to make only one, remember to triple the ingredients.

Spinach-and-Garlic Sauce

Makes about ¼ litre (8 fl oz)
Working (and total) time: about 15 minutes

Calories **20**
Protein **1g**
Cholesterol **0mg**
Total fat **2g**
Saturated fat **0g**
Sodium **85mg**

500 g	*spinach, washed and stemmed*	*1 lb*
1 tbsp	*safflower oil*	*1 tbsp*
2	*garlic cloves, finely chopped*	*2*
15 cl	*fish stock (recipe, page 136)*	*¼ pint*
¼ tsp	*salt*	*¼ tsp*
⅛ tsp	*white pepper*	*⅛ tsp*
	pinch of nutmeg	

Place the spinach, with just the water that clings to its leaves, in a large saucepan over high heat. Cover the pan and steam the spinach until it is wilted — 1 to 2 minutes. Drain it well. Squeeze the spinach with your hands to rid it of excess liquid, then chop the spinach coarsely and set it aside.

Heat the oil in a small saucepan over medium heat. Add the garlic and cook it for about 30 seconds. Add the spinach, stock, salt, pepper and nutmeg, and simmer the mixture for 3 minutes. Transfer the mixture to a food processor or blender and purée it. Pour the sauce into a serving bowl. Serve the sauce warm with the poached salmon.

Radish-and-Ginger Sauce

Makes about ¼ litre (8 fl oz)
Working time: about 15 minutes
Total time: about 25 minutes

Calories **40**
Protein **1g**
Cholesterol **5mg**
Total fat **3g**
Saturated fat **1g**
Sodium **80mg**

1 tbsp	*safflower oil*	*1 tbsp*
1	*small onion, finely chopped*	*1*
2 tbsp	*finely chopped fresh ginger root*	*2 tbsp*
250 g	*daikon radish, peeled and thinly sliced*	*8 oz*
12.5 cl	*fish stock (recipe, page 136)*	*4 fl oz*
¼ tsp	*salt*	*¼ tsp*
⅛ tsp	*white pepper*	*⅛ tsp*
4 tbsp	*soured cream*	*4 tbsp*
4 tbsp	*plain low-fat yogurt*	*4 tbsp*

Heat the oil in small saucepan over medium heat. Add the onion and cook it, stirring occasionally, until it is transparent — 3 to 4 minutes. Stir in the ginger and cook for 1 minute more. Add the radish and the stock; simmer the mixture, partially covered, until the radish is tender — about 10 minutes.

Transfer the mixture to a food processor or blender and purée it. Add an additional tablespoon of stock or water, if necessary, to achieve a smooth consistency. Transfer the purée to a bowl and stir in the salt and pepper, then fold in the soured cream and the yogurt. Spoon the sauce into a serving bowl and serve it with the poached salmon.

Plum Sauce with Chutney

Makes about ¼ litre (8 fl oz)
Working (and total) time: about 15 minutes

Calories **50**
Protein **0g**
Cholesterol **0mg**
Total fat **0g**
Saturated fat **0g**
Sodium **20mg**

350 g	*red plums, halved and stoned*	*12 oz*
4 tbsp	*mango chutney*	*4 tbsp*
4 tbsp	*dry white wine*	*4 tbsp*

Combine the plums, chutney and wine in a small saucepan over medium-low heat, and bring the liquid to a simmer. Cover the pan and cook the mixture until the plums have softened — about 7 minutes. Transfer the mixture to a food processor or blender and purée it. Pour the sauce into a serving bowl. Serve the sauce with the poached salmon.

Soufflé of Smoked Trout

Serves 6
Working time: about 30 minutes
Total time: about 1 hour and 20 minutes

Calories **225**
Protein **24g**
Cholesterol **145mg**
Total fat **9g**
Saturated fat **3g**
Sodium **305mg**

1	*small smoked trout fillet, skinned and boned, the flesh shredded (about 60 g/2 oz)*	1
4	*freshwater trout, filleted (about 500 g/l lb of fillets; page 130) or 500 g (1 lb) sea trout fillets*	4
2 tbsp	*finely cut fresh dill*	2 tbsp
2 tbsp	*fresh lemon juice*	2 tbsp
15 g	*unsalted butter*	½ oz
1	*onion, finely chopped*	1
6 tbsp	*plain flour*	6 tbsp
¼ litre	*skimmed milk*	8 fl oz
¼ litre	*fish stock (recipe, page 136), or an additional ¼ litre (8 fl oz) skimmed milk*	8 fl oz
¼ tsp	*fresh thyme, or ⅛ tsp dried thyme*	¼ tsp
⅛ tsp	*grated nutmeg*	⅛ tsp
¼ tsp	*salt*	¼ tsp
	freshly ground black pepper	
2	*egg yolks*	2
8	*egg whites*	8
⅛ tsp	*cream of tartar*	⅛ tsp

Preheat the oven to 220°C (425°F or Mark 7). Rinse the fresh trout fillets under cold running water and pat them dry with paper towels. Wrap the fillets in a single piece of aluminium foil, its dull side out, and set the foil package on a baking sheet. Bake the fillets until they are opaque — approximately 15 minutes.

Unwrap the fillets and spread them out to cool. Flake the flesh with a fork, carefully picking out all the bones. In a large bowl, combine the fresh trout with the smoked trout, the dill and the lemon juice. Set the fish mixture aside.

Melt the butter in a heavy-bottomed saucepan over medium-high heat. Add the onion and cook it until it is translucent — about 4 minutes. While the onion is cooking, put the flour in a bowl and stir in the milk and the stock, if you are using it. Pour this mixture into the saucepan and bring it to the boil, whisking constantly. Remove the pan from the heat and whisk in the thyme,

nutmeg, salt, pepper and egg yolks; set the mixture aside and keep it warm.

Put the egg whites in a bowl with the cream of tartar; with a whisk or an electric mixer, beat the egg whites into stiff peaks. Stir the milk-and-stock mixture into the fish mixture. Stir about one quarter of the egg whites into the fish mixture, then gently fold in the remaining whites.

Pour the mixture into a lightly buttered 2 litre (3½ pint) soufflé dish; the mixture should come to within 1 cm (½ inch) of the rim. Put the dish in the oven. Immediately reduce the oven temperature to 190°C (375°F or Mark 5). Bake the soufflé until it is puffed and golden and the centre has set — about 45 minutes. Serve immediately.

SUGGESTED ACCOMPANIMENT: *chicory and radicchio salad.*

Cucumber-Stuffed Trout with Dill Sauce

Serves 4
Working time: about 30 minutes
Total time: about 40 minutes

Calories **440**
Protein **29g**
Cholesterol **80mg**
Total fat **23g**
Saturated fat **4g**
Sodium **430mg**

4	*rainbow trout (about 250 g/8 oz) each (or redfish or Norway haddock), cleaned, scaled and filleted (page 130), the skin left on*	*4*
2½ tbsp	*safflower oil*	*2½ tbsp*
250 g	*cucumber, peeled and thinly sliced*	*8 oz*
1 tbsp	*finely chopped shallot*	*1 tbsp*
¼ tsp	*salt*	*¼ tsp*
	freshly ground black pepper	
4 tbsp	*dry vermouth*	*4 tbsp*
60 g	*flour*	*2 oz*
2	*egg whites, lightly beaten*	*2*
100 g	*dry breadcrumbs*	*3½ oz*
	dill sprigs for garnish	
	Dill sauce	
75 g	*finely cut fresh dill*	*2½ oz*
¼ litre	*plain low-fat yogurt*	*8 fl oz*
1 tbsp	*dried dill*	*1 tbsp*
2 tbsp	*finely chopped shallot*	*2 tbsp*
⅛ tsp	*salt*	*⅛ tsp*
⅛ tsp	*white pepper*	*⅛ tsp*

Preheat the oven to 190°C (375°F or Mark 5).

Pour ½ tablespoon of the oil into a large, shallow fireproof casserole over medium-high heat. Add the cucumber and sauté it until it begins to soften —about 2 minutes. Add the shallot and cook it, stirring constantly, until it turns translucent — 1 to 2 minutes. Reduce the heat to low; season the vegetables with ⅛ teaspoon of the salt and some black pepper. Pour in the vermouth and simmer the mixture until nearly all the liquid has evaporated — about 3 minutes. Remove the casserole from the heat and set it aside.

To prepare the dill sauce, fold the cut fresh dill into the yogurt with the dried dill, shallot, salt and white pepper.

Lay one half of each filleted fish skin side down on a work surface. Season the fish with some black pepper and the remaining salt. Arrange a layer of cucumber slices on each half, reserving a few slices for garnish. Lay the remaining fillets on their respective halves to form fish packets.

Holding a fish packet together like a sandwich, press each side first into the flour, then into the egg white, and last into the breadcrumbs. Wipe out the casserole, set it over medium heat and pour in the remaining oil. Fry the fish packets on one side until they are lightly browned — about 2 minutes. Turn them over and transfer the casserole to the oven; bake the fish until they can be easily flaked with a fork at the thickest point — 4 to 5 minutes.

Carefully transfer the fish to a warm platter. Spoon some of the dill sauce over each fish packet. Garnish the packets with the reserved cucumber slices and the dill sprigs; serve the remaining sauce on the side.

EDITOR'S NOTE: *The dried dill in this recipe is used to intensify the flavour of the fresh dill.*

Grilled Trout and Dried Figs

Serves 4
Working time: about 1 hour
Total time: about 1 hour and 10 minutes

Calories **435**
Protein **33g**
Cholesterol **95mg**
Total fat **11g**
Saturated fat **2g**
Sodium **255mg**

4	*trout, about 350 g (12 oz) each, cleaned, the fins removed*	4
12	*dried figs, halved lengthwise*	12
¼ litre	*medium-dry sherry*	8 fl oz
3 tbsp	*balsamic vinegar or sherry vinegar*	3 tbsp
1 tbsp	*maple syrup or honey*	1 tbsp
1 tbsp	*Dijon mustard*	1 tbsp
¼ tsp	*salt*	¼ tsp
	freshly ground black pepper	

Put the figs in a non-reactive saucepan over low heat with the sherry and 2 tablespoons of the vinegar. Simmer the figs for 10 minutes. Remove the pan from the heat and let the figs steep in the liquid.

While the figs are steeping, butterfly the trout, as follows. Cut off and discard the heads of the trout. With a small, sharp knife, cut through the back of a trout on one side of its backbone from the head to within 2.5 cm (1 inch) of the tail. Repeat the cutting procedure on the other side of the backbone. Using kitchen scissors, sever the backbone near the tail; lift it out with your fingers. With tweezers, pull out any small bones remaining in the trout. Rinse the fish under cold running water, then pat it dry with paper towels. Repeat these steps to butterfly the remaining trout.

Preheat the grill. Remove the figs from their steeping liquid and set them aside. Stir the maple syrup or honey into the liquid, then cook the liquid over medium heat until only about 6 tablespoons remains — approximately 5 minutes. Whisk the mustard and the remaining vinegar into the sauce. Remove the pan from the heat.

Set the butterflied trout, skin side down, on a grill pan and tuck their sides under slightly. Sprinkle the fish with the salt and pepper and brush them with about half of the sauce. Grill the trout 7.5 cm (3 inches) below the heat source until their flesh is opaque — about 5 minutes. Put the figs on the grill pan with the fish. Brush the fish and figs with the remaining sauce and grill them together for 1 minute before serving.

SUGGESTED ACCOMPANIMENT: *stir-fried carrots.*

Poached Trout with Horseradish Sauce

Serves 4
Working time: about 45 minutes
Total time: about 3 hours and 45 minutes

Calories **265**
Protein **42g**
Cholesterol **90mg**
Total fat **11g**
Saturated fat **2g**
Sodium **190mg**

4	*trout (250 to 350 g/8 to 12 oz each), gutted, fins removed*	4
60 cl	*court-bouillon (recipe, page 136)*	1 pint
	Horseradish sauce	
1 tbsp	*finely grated fresh horseradish, or 2 tsp prepared horseradish*	1 tbsp
1 tbsp	*lemon juice*	1 tbsp
1 tsp	*Dijon mustard*	1 tsp
12.5 cl	*soured cream*	4 fl oz
	freshly ground black pepper	
	Garnish	
	thinly sliced radishes	
	fresh herbs (chervil, tarragon or chives)	
	lemon slices	
	finely shredded lettuce leaves	

Wash the trout thoroughly under cold running water then pat them dry with paper towels.

Pour the court-bouillon into a wide shallow saucepan and bring it to the boil. Place the trout in a single layer in the court-bouillon, ensuring that they are well covered. Cover the saucepan, reduce the heat to low and simmer for 10 minutes. Remove from the heat and allow the trout to cool in the court-bouillon until quite cold (overnight, if desired).

Meanwhile, make the sauce. Blend the horseradish with the remaining ingredients in a small bowl. Pour the sauce into a serving bowl, cover and refrigerate until ready to serve.

Lift the trout from the court-bouillon on to a large wire rack placed over a tray. Very carefully remove the skin from the top side of each fish. Garnish decoratively with radishes, fresh herbs and lemon slices.

Place the trout on a large serving dish, or individual plates, and surround them with finely shredded lettuce leaves. Serve with the horseradish sauce.

SUGGESTED ACCOMPANIMENT: *salad of sliced artichoke hearts and asparagus.*

Mackerel Brochettes

Serves 4
Working time: about 45 minutes
Total time: about 1 hour and 45 minutes

Calories **485**
Protein **31g**
Cholesterol **135mg**
Total fat **20g**
Saturated fat **4g**
Sodium **220mg**

500 g	*mackerel fillets (or salmon or tuna steaks)*	1 lb
1	*fennel bulb, base cut into 1 cm (½ inch) squares, feathery tops reserved*	1
8	*pearl onions, unpeeled*	8
1	*garlic clove*	1
⅛ tsp	*salt*	⅛ tsp
1	*lemon, juice only*	1
12.5 cl	*dry white wine*	4 fl oz
1 tsp	*fresh thyme, or ½ tsp dried thyme*	1 tsp
8	*cherry tomatoes*	8
1	*medium courgette, sliced into 2 cm (¾ inch) thick slices*	1
8	*button mushrooms, wiped clean*	8
250 g	*fresh spinach fettuccine*	8 oz
	Peppery tomato sauce	
1 tbsp	*virgin olive oil*	1 tbsp
2	*shallots, finely chopped*	2
2	*garlic cloves, finely chopped*	2
1.25 kg	*ripe tomatoes, skinned, seeded and coarsely chopped*	2½ lb
1 tsp	*fresh thyme, or ½ tsp dried thyme*	1 tsp
⅛ tsp	*salt*	⅛ tsp
⅛ tsp	*cayenne pepper*	⅛ tsp
	freshly ground black pepper	

Rinse the fillets under cold running water and pat them dry with paper towels. Cut the fish into chunks about 2.5 cm (1 inch) thick.

Cook the fennel squares in boiling water for 3 minutes. Remove the fennel with a slotted spoon. Parboil the pearl onions for 3 minutes; when they are cool enough to handle, peel them.

To prepare the marinade, pound together the garlic and salt into a paste in a large bowl. Stir in the lemon juice, wine and thyme. Finely chop enough of the feathery fennel tops to yield 1 tablespoon and add them to the marinade; reserve the remaining tops for garnish. Add the fish, fennel squares, pearl onions, cherry tomatoes, courgette and mushrooms to the bowl. Stir gently to coat the fish and vegetables. Refrigerate for 1 hour, stirring from time to time.

To make the sauce, heat the oil in a large, heavy frying pan over low heat. Add the shallots and garlic, and cook them, stirring occasionally, until the shallots are soft — about 5 minutes. Stir in the tomatoes, then the thyme, salt, cayenne pepper and some black pepper. Cook the sauce for 15 minutes, then, using a wooden spoon, push the sauce through a sieve into a small saucepan and keep it warm.

Preheat the grill or barbecue. Put 3 litres (5 pints) of water on to boil with 1½ teaspoons of salt. Thread the fish and vegetables on to eight long skewers. Cook the brochettes, turning occasionally, until the fish is browned and the vegetables are tender — 8 to 10 minutes. While the brochettes are cooking, add the fettuccine to the boiling water. Start testing the fettuccine after 2 minutes and cook it until it is *al dente*. Drain the pasta and toss it with the tomato sauce.

Divide the pasta evenly between four plates; place two brochettes on each plate. Garnish the servings with the reserved fennel tops and serve immediately.

Mackerel Fillets with Rhubarb Sauce

Serves 4
Working time: about 10 minutes
Total time: about 40 minutes

Calories **325**
Protein **22g**
Cholesterol **90mg**
Total fat **16g**
Saturated fat **3g**
Sodium **175mg**

500 g	*mackerel fillets, skin left on*	*1 lb*
2 tbsp	*sugar*	*2 tbsp*
1 tbsp	*red wine vinegar*	*1 tbsp*
2	*navel oranges, the julienned rind and juice of one reserved, the other peeled and sliced into thin rounds*	*2*
250 g	*rhubarb, thinly sliced*	*8 oz*
⅛ tsp	*ground cumin*	*⅛ tsp*
¼ tsp	*salt*	*¼ tsp*
	freshly ground black pepper	
1 tbsp	*safflower oil*	*1 tbsp*

In a small, heavy-bottomed non-reactive saucepan over high heat, cook the sugar, stirring constantly with a wooden spoon, until it melts and forms a syrup. Cook the syrup, stirring all the while, until it turns a light caramel colour — 30 seconds to 1 minute. (If the sugar turns dark brown, discard it and start again.) Standing well back to avoid being splattered, immediately pour in the vinegar and orange juice; the sugar will harden. Reduce the heat to medium low and cook the mixture until it becomes syrupy again — 3 to 5 minutes.

Add the orange rind, rhubarb, cumin and ⅛ teaspoon of the salt to the saucepan. Cover the pan and cook the mixture until the rhubarb is soft and has begun to lose its shape — about 15 minutes. Purée the mixture through a sieve or in a blender. If you are using a blender, sieve the rhubarb after it has been puréed.

While the rhubarb is cooking, preheat the grill. Rinse the fillets under cold running water and pat them dry with paper towels. Sprinkle the remaining salt and some pepper over the skinless side of the fillets. Place the fish skin side down on a baking sheet and brush the tops with the oil. Grill the fillets about 8.5 cm (3½ inches) below the heat source for 6 minutes, then turn the fillets skin side up and cook them for 2 minutes more. To test for doneness, insert a fork into a fillet at its thickest point; the flesh should be opaque all the way through.

Gently transfer the fillets to a serving platter, add the rhubarb sauce and garnish with the orange slices.

SUGGESTED ACCOMPANIMENT: *sautéed mushrooms.*

Grilled Freshwater Bream

Serves 4
Working time: about 30 minutes
Total time: about 1 hour and 10 minutes

Calories **290**
Protein **44g**
Cholesterol **90mg**
Total fat **12g**
Saturated fat **1g**
Sodium **360mg**

2	*freshwater bream (about 750 g/1½ lb each)*	2
1 tbsp	*virgin olive oil*	*1 tbsp*
1 tsp	*green peppercorns, crushed*	*1 tsp*
	fresh rosemary sprigs	
	fresh thyme sprigs	
½ tsp	*salt*	*½ tsp*
	lemon wedges for garnish	

Remove the fins, scales and viscera, but not the head, from the bream, as demonstrated on pages 128-129. Wash the fish well under cold running water, then pat them dry with paper towels. Make two or three deep slashes in the sides of each bream. Rub the olive oil and the crushed peppercorns over the bream, then press sprigs of fresh rosemary and thyme into the slashes. Season the fish with the salt.

Put the fish on a dish, cover them and let them stand for 30 minutes.

Heat the grill to high. Place the fish in a fish grill, or on a rack in the grill pan. Grill for 4 to 5 minutes on each side, until the flesh flakes easily. Garnish with lemon wedges and serve immediately.

Alternatively, the bream can be baked in an oven preheated to 200°C (400°F or Mark 6): place the fish in an ovenproof dish and bake uncovered for 25 minutes until cooked.

SUGGESTED ACCOMPANIMENT: *curly endive and orange salad.*

Baked Trout Stuffed with Kumquats and Spring Greens

Serves 8
Working time: about 45 minutes
Total time: about 1 hour and 15 minutes

Calories **290**
Protein **24g**
Cholesterol **50mg**
Total fat **18g**
Saturated fat **4g**
Sodium **280mg**

2.5 kg	*trout (or sea trout or salmon), scaled and filleted, skin left on (pages 128, 130)*	*5 lb*
2	*garlic cloves, finely chopped*	*2*
2 tbsp	*fresh lemon juice*	*2 tbsp*
¾ tsp	*salt*	*¾ tsp*
	freshly ground black pepper	
30 g	*unsalted butter*	*1 oz*
2 tbsp	*safflower oil*	*2 tbsp*
2	*medium leeks, trimmed, split, washed thoroughly to remove any grit, and thinly sliced*	*2*
1½ tsp	*fresh thyme, or ½ tsp dried thyme*	*1½ tsp*
125 g	*fresh kumquats, thinly sliced and seeded*	*4 oz*
350 g	*spring greens, washed, stemmed and chopped*	*12 oz*
45 g	*dry breadcrumbs*	*1½ oz*

Run your fingers over the fillets to locate any small bones; using tweezers, carefully pull out the bones. Rinse the fillets under cold running water and pat them dry with paper towels. Rub the fillets with the garlic, lemon juice, ½ teaspoon of the salt and some pepper. Set the fillets aside while you prepare the stuffing.

Preheat the oven to 190°C (375°F or Mark 5). Put the butter and 1 tablespoon of the oil in a large, heavy frying pan over medium heat. When the butter has melted, add the leeks and thyme; cook, stirring occasionally, for 5 minutes. Stir in the kumquats and cook for 2 minutes more. Add the spring greens, the remaining salt and some more pepper. Cook the mixture until the spring greens are wilted and tender — 5 to 7 minutes. Stir in the breadcrumbs and remove the pan from the heat.

Lay one of the fish fillets skin side down in a large, lightly oiled baking dish. Spread the greens-kumquat mixture over the fillet. Lay the remaining fillet skin side up on the stuffing. Brush the remaining oil over the top of the fish.

Bake the assembly until the fillets are opaque and the filling is hot — 25 to 30 minutes. Carefully transfer the fish to a serving platter, slice, and serve.

SUGGESTED ACCOMPANIMENT: *baked potatoes with chives.*

3 *A harvest of scallops, clams, lobsters, crayfish, crabs, oysters and mussels suggests the abundance of European waters.*

Shellfish's Manifold Pleasures

Shellfish, which abound along the margins of the oceans in an almost unbelievable variety, are savoured the world over. They can be conveniently grouped into three basic categories. The common bivalve molluscs include the clam, oyster and mussel. Among the crustaceans are prawn, lobster, crab and crayfish. Octopus and squid, though molluscs, have no outer shells and belong to a group called the cephalopods.

While most molluscs and crustaceans have slightly less protein than finned fish, they are well endowed with minerals. Like tiny biological factories, they concentrate vital trace elements from sea water — iron, copper, iodine and zinc, among others. Recent findings suggest that the presence of plant sterols in clams, oysters and mussels helps to reduce bodily absorption of the cholesterol they do contain. Squid, octopus and prawns, on the other hand, contain relatively high levels of cholesterol.

The one essential in shellfish cookery is absolute freshness. The freshest clams, mussels and oysters are sold live in their shells — which means that they must be cleaned and shucked at home *(page 95)*. To reduce the risk of eating contaminated shellfish, be sure to buy them from a reliable fishmonger.

Shellfish can be served in limitless ways. Oysters and some clams may be eaten raw or, like mussels, they may be steamed in their shells, with results that are both healthy and mouth watering. Scallops, sold either on their open shells or without shells, lend themselves readily to steaming, sautéing, grilling and baking. But as with all bivalves, care must be taken to avoid overcooking them. A scallop — or a clam or oyster, for that matter — cooked for more than a minute or two will turn rubbery.

The shell-less molluscs each require different cooking strategies. A small piece of cartilage, known as a pen or quill, runs through the squid's body, and this must be removed, along with the ink sac, before cooking *(page 132)*. The flesh of squid and octopus is tender, especially that of smaller specimens. It can be stir-fried quickly, but it toughens after a few minutes over heat; then, if cooked longer, as in the squid stew with red wine on page 110, it will soften again. Squid can be scored with a knife to make its meat more supple. Many cooks recommend pounding larger squid and octopus with a mallet to tenderize them before cooking.

Steaming and poaching are the classic techniques for handling crustaceans. They may also be grilled or barbecued, or the meat stir-fried with vegetables. The 28 recipes that follow explore all these methods.

Dressed Crab with Prawn and Yogurt Sauce

Serves 4
Working (and total) time: about 1 hour

Calories **230**
Protein **25g**
Cholesterol **100mg**
Total fat **11**
Saturated fat **3g**
Sodium **455mg**

2	*cooked crabs (about 1 kg/2½ lb each)*	*2*
	Prawn and yogurt sauce	
15 g	*fresh ginger root, peeled*	*½ oz*
175 g	*peeled cooked prawns*	*6 oz*
15 cl	*plain yogurt*	*5 fl oz*
1 tbsp	*lemon juice*	*1 tbsp*
¼ tsp	*salt*	*¼ tsp*
	freshly ground black pepper	
1 tbsp	*chopped chives*	*1 tbsp*
	Garnish	
2 tbsp	*chopped chives*	*2 tbsp*
½ tsp	*paprika*	*½ tsp*
	lettuce leaves	
	lemon slices or wedges	

Prepare the crabs as demonstrated on page 133, keeping the white and brown meats separate.

Neaten the empty crab shells by breaking away the thin part of the shell on the underside, following the natural curved line. Wash the shells thoroughly and dry well.

Fill the crab shells with the crab meat, placing the white meat to the sides, and the brown meat down the centre. Garnish with neat lines of chopped chives and paprika. Refrigerate while making the sauce.

To make the sauce, chop the ginger very finely. Put a few peeled prawns aside for garnish and roughly chop the rest. Blend the yogurt with the lemon juice, salt, pepper and 1 tablespoon of chopped chives, then stir in the ginger and prawns. Spoon the sauce into a serving bowl. Garnish it with a light sprinkling of chives, paprika and the reserved prawns.

Line a serving dish with lettuce leaves, place the crab shells on the dish, then garnish with the lemon slices. Serve the crabs accompanied by the sauce.

Asian Crab and Vegetable Salad

Serves 6 as a luncheon salad
Working time: about 35 minutes
Total time: about 1 hour

Calories **165**
Protein **15g**
Cholesterol **60mg**
Total fat **6g**
Saturated fat **1g**
Sodium **250mg**

500 g	*white crab meat, picked over*	*1 lb*
1	*lemon, juice only*	*1*
¼ tsp	*salt*	*¼ tsp*
	freshly ground black pepper	
1 tsp	*dry mustard*	*1 tsp*
2 tbsp	*chopped fresh ginger root*	*2 tbsp*
2 tsp	*rice vinegar*	*2 tsp*
1	*garlic clove, finely chopped*	*1*
2 tbsp	*dry white wine*	*2 tbsp*
2 tbsp	*groundnut oil*	*2 tbsp*
¼ tsp	*dark sesame oil*	*¼ tsp*
175 g	*cucumber, peeled, seeded and sliced, the slices quartered*	*6 oz*
250 g	*fresh bamboo shoots, sliced, blanched for 1 minute and drained, or canned bamboo shoots, sliced, blanched for 10 seconds and drained*	*8 oz*
250 g	*fresh water chestnuts, peeled and sliced, blanched for 1 minute and drained, or canned water chestnuts, drained, sliced*	*8 oz*
125 g	*mange-tout, strings removed, julienned*	*4 oz*
2 tbsp	*chopped pimiento*	*2 tbsp*
2	*round lettuces, leaves washed and patted dry*	*2*

In a large bowl, combine the crab meat with the lemon juice, ⅛ teaspoon of the salt and some pepper. Refrigerate the mixture while you assemble the remaining ingredients for the salad.

To make the dressing, first put the mustard in a bowl. Place the ginger in a piece of muslin and squeeze it over the bowl to extract the juice; discard the ginger. Pour in the vinegar and whisk well, then add the garlic and wine, and whisk again. Let the mixture stand for 5 minutes before whisking in the groundnut oil and sesame oil. Add the remaining salt and some more pepper. Set the dressing aside.

Add the cucumber, bamboo shoots, water chestnuts, mange-tout and pimiento to the crab meat, and mix well. Pour the dressing over the salad and toss gently. Chill the salad for 30 minutes.

To serve, arrange the lettuce leaves on individual serving plates. Spoon the salad into the leaves and serve immediately.

Crab-Stuffed Mushroom Caps

Serves 12 as an hors d'oeuvre
Working time: about 25 minutes
Total time: about 50 minutes

Calories **100**
Protein **8g**
Cholesterol **20mg**
Total fat **4g**
Saturated fat **2g**
Sodium **135mg**

250 g	*crab meat, picked over*	*8 oz*
35 cl	*fish stock (recipe, page 136)*	*12 fl oz*
1	*lemon, juice only*	*1*
36	*large mushrooms (about 1.25 kg/ 2½ lb), wiped clean, stems carefully removed and finely chopped*	*36*
2 tbsp	*finely chopped shallot*	*2 tbsp*
12.5 cl	*dry vermouth*	*4 fl oz*
2 tsp	*fresh thyme, or ½ tsp dried thyme*	*2 tsp*
15 g	*unsalted butter*	*½ oz*
2 tbsp	*flour*	*2 tbsp*
17.5 cl	*semi-skimmed milk*	*6 fl oz*
⅛ tsp	*salt*	*⅛ tsp*
	grated nutmeg	
	white pepper	
60 g	*Parmesan cheese, freshly grated*	*2 oz*
15 g	*fresh basil, coarsely chopped*	*½ oz*
2 tbsp	*unsalted pistachio nuts, crushed*	*2 tbsp*

In a large, non-reactive frying pan, heat ¼ litre (8 fl oz) of the stock and the lemon juice over medium heat. Add the mushroom caps and toss them gently to coat them with the liquid. Cover the pan and poach the mushrooms, turning them occasionally to ensure even cooking, until they are cooked through — 6 to 7 minutes.

With a slotted spoon, transfer the mushrooms to a platter lined with paper towels. Add the shallot to the pan along with the chopped mushroom stems, the vermouth and the thyme. Bring the liquid to the boil, then reduce the heat to medium and cook the mixture at a brisk simmer, stirring occasionally, until all but 2 tablespoons of the liquid has evaporated — about 15 minutes. Set the mushroom mixture aside.

Melt the butter in a small saucepan over medium heat. Whisk in the flour to form a paste, and cook the paste for 3 minutes. Stirring constantly to prevent lumps from forming, slowly pour in the milk, then the remaining stock. Add the salt and sprinkle in some nutmeg and white pepper. Simmer the sauce until it thickens — about 3 minutes. Stir in the cheese and the basil.

Preheat the grill. To complete the filling, combine the crab meat with the mushroom mixture in a bowl. Slowly pour the sauce into the bowl and stir gently to coat the stuffing. Mound ¾ tablespoon of stuffing in the hollow of each mushroom cap. Grill the stuffed mushrooms 7.5 cm (3 inches) below the heat source until the crab begins to brown — about 3 minutes. Sprinkle the pistachios over the top of the mushrooms and serve them hot.

Scallops in Fermented Black Bean Sauce

Serves 4
Working (and total) time: 15 minutes

Calories **185**
Protein **20g**
Cholesterol **40mg**
Total fat **7g**
Saturated fat **1g**
Sodium **235mg**

500 g	*shelled queen scallops*	*1 lb*
2 tbsp	*apricot jam or orange marmalade*	*2 tbsp*
4 tbsp	*fresh lime juice*	*4 tbsp*
1½ tbsp	*fermented black beans, rinsed*	*1½ tbsp*
1 tbsp	*chopped fresh ginger root*	*1 tbsp*
	freshly ground black pepper	
1½ tbsp	*safflower oil*	*1½ tbsp*

To prepare the sauce, combine the jam or marmalade, lime juice, black beans, ginger and some pepper in a small bowl. Set the sauce aside.

Rinse the scallops under cold running water. Heat the oil in a large, heavy frying pan over high heat. When the oil is hot, add the scallops and cook them, stirring constantly, for 1 minute. Add the sauce and continue cooking, stirring all the while, for 1 minute more. With a slotted spoon, transfer the scallops to a heated platter. Cook the sauce, stirring, until it is reduced by half — 1 to 2 minutes. Pour the sauce over the scallops and serve immediately.

SUGGESTED ACCOMPANIMENT: *green beans.*

Crab-Potato Cakes

Serves 6 (makes 12 cakes)
Working time: about 30 minutes
Total time: about 1 hour

Calories **215**
Protein **17g**
Cholesterol **65mg**
Total fat **8g**
Saturated fat **2g**
Sodium **300mg**

500 g	*crab meat, picked over*	*1 lb*
500 g	*potatoes, boiled, cooled, peeled and coarsely grated*	*1 lb*
125 g	*onion, finely chopped*	*4 oz*
30 g	*fresh parsley, finely chopped*	*1 oz*
3 tbsp	*finely cut dill*	*3 tbsp*
1 tbsp	*dry sherry*	*1 tbsp*
2 tbsp	*plain low-fat yogurt*	*2 tbsp*
2	*egg whites, beaten*	*2*
¼ tsp	*salt*	*¼ tsp*
¼ tsp	*freshly ground black pepper*	*¼ tsp*
¼ tsp	*ground mace*	*¼ tsp*
⅛ tsp	*cayenne pepper*	*⅛ tsp*
75 g	*dry breadcrumbs*	*2½ oz*
15 g	*unsalted butter*	*½ oz*
2 tbsp	*safflower oil*	*2 tbsp*
	parsley sprigs for garnish	
2	*lemons, cut into wedges*	*2*

Preheat the grill. In a large mixing bowl, combine the crab meat, potatoes, onion, chopped parsley, dill, sherry, yogurt, egg whites, salt, pepper, mace and cayenne pepper; mix gently until the ingredients are thoroughly combined.

Form the mixture into 12 cakes, each about 1 cm (½ inch) thick. Dredge each cake in the breadcrumbs to coat it completely. Put the cakes on a lightly buttered grill pan as you work. Melt the butter and oil together; dribble half of this mixture over the tops of the cakes.

Grill the cakes until they turn a crusty golden-brown — 3 to 5 minutes. Turn the cakes over and dribble the remaining butter mixture over them. Grill the cakes for 3 to 5 minutes more. Serve immediately, garnished with the parsley sprigs and the lemon wedges.

SUGGESTED ACCOMPANIMENT: *steamed julienned carrots and courgettes with fresh herbs.*

Chilled Scallops and Asparagus

Serves 4
Working time: about 45 minutes
Total time: about 1 hour

Calories **205**
Protein **15g**
Cholesterol **30mg**
Total fat **11g**
Saturated fat **1g**
Sodium **210mg**

350 g	*shelled scallops, bright white connective tissue removed*	*12 oz*
1 tbsp	*safflower oil*	*1 tbsp*
1½ tsp	*fresh lime juice*	*1½ tsp*
¼ tsp	*salt*	*¼ tsp*
350 g	*asparagus, trimmed and julienned*	*12 oz*
1	*navel orange, peeled and cut into sections*	*1*
	Onion-orange vinaigrette	
3	*spring onions, trimmed and finely chopped*	*3*
1	*orange, juice only*	*1*
1½ tbsp	*red wine vinegar*	*1½ tbsp*
½ tsp	*sugar*	*½ tsp*
1 tsp	*fresh thyme, or ¼ tsp dried thyme*	*1 tsp*
1 tbsp	*julienned orange rind*	*1 tbsp*
1 tbsp	*virgin olive oil*	*1 tbsp*
1 tbsp	*safflower oil*	*1 tbsp*

To make the vinaigrette, combine the spring onions with the orange juice, vinegar, sugar, thyme and orange rind in a small bowl. Let the mixture stand for at least 10 minutes, then whisk in the olive oil and safflower oil. Set the vinaigrette aside.

Rinse the scallops under cold running water. If you are using large scallops, cut them into thin strips; if you are using queen scallops, cut each one in half horizontally. Set the scallops aside.

Put 2 litres (3½ pints) of water on to boil in a large saucepan. Meanwhile, pour the tablespoon of safflower oil into a heavy frying pan over medium-low heat. When the oil is hot, add the scallops, lime juice and salt, and stir gently until the scallops turn pearl white — about 1 minute. Transfer the scallops to a bowl and refrigerate them until cool — at least 10 minutes.

Blanch the asparagus in the boiling water for 15 seconds; drain it and refresh it under cold running water. Transfer the asparagus to a plate lined with paper towels and refrigerate it.

To serve, drain the liquid from the scallops and gently toss them with the cold asparagus and the vinaigrette. Divide the mixture between individual plates; garnish each serving with a few orange sections.

EDITOR'S NOTE: *This dish is an ideal main course for a summer lunch. It may also be served as an appetizer at dinner.*

Crayfish Boil

Serves 4 as a first course
Working time: about 10 minutes
Total time: about 25 minutes

Calories **100**
Protein **19g**
Cholesterol **180mg**
Total fat **0g**
Saturated fat **0g**
Sodium **65mg**

2.5 kg	*live crayfish*	*5 lb*
4	*onions, sliced*	*4*
2	*dried chili peppers*	*2*
1	*whole bulb of garlic, cut in half horizontally*	*1*
15 g	*fresh thyme, or 2 tbsp dried thyme*	*½ oz*
15 g	*fresh rosemary, or 2 tbsp dried rosemary*	*½ oz*
15 g	*fresh sage, or 2 tbsp dried sage*	*½ oz*
1 tbsp	*dill seeds*	*1 tbsp*
1 tbsp	*celery seeds*	*1 tbsp*
12.5 cl	*cider vinegar*	*4 fl oz*

To prepare the crayfish, immerse them in cold water for 10 minutes, then rinse the crayfish well under cold running water.

Pour 6 litres (10 pints) of water into a large stockpot. Add the onions, chili peppers, garlic, thyme, rosemary, sage, dill seeds, celery seeds and vinegar, and bring the water to the boil. Add all the crayfish to the pot, tightly cover it, and return the water to the boil. Cook the crayfish for 5 minutes, then transfer them to a large platter. Serve the crayfish hot or cold, in their shells, and provide each guest with a liberal supply of paper napkins.

EDITOR'S NOTE: *The technique of eating boiled crayfish is easily mastered. Break the tail from the body, then split the tail shell lengthwise and remove the meat with your fingers. Crack the larger claws with your teeth and suck out the delicate morsel within.*

Ragout of Scallops and Red Peppers

Serves 4
Working (and total) time: about 45 minutes

Calories **225**
Protein **21g**
Cholesterol **40mg**
Total fat **8g**
Saturated fat **1g**
Sodium **250mg**

500 g	*shelled scallops, bright white connective tissue removed*	*1 lb*
2	*sweet red peppers*	*2*
	freshly ground black pepper	
1 tbsp	*fresh lime juice*	*1 tbsp*
2 tbsp	*red wine vinegar*	*2 tbsp*
2 tsp	*fresh thyme, or ½ tsp dried thyme*	*2 tsp*
2 tbsp	*virgin olive oil*	*2 tbsp*
250 g	*mushrooms, wiped clean and quartered*	*8 oz*
¼ tsp	*salt*	*¼ tsp*
12.5 cl	*dry white wine*	*4 fl oz*
1	*bunch spring onions, trimmed and cut into 2.5 cm (1 inch) pieces*	*1*
150 g	*chicory, cut into 2.5 cm (1 inch) pieces, pieces separated*	*5 oz*

Roast the peppers about 7.5 cm (3 inches) below a preheated grill, turning them occasionally until they are blackened all over — about 15 minutes.

Meanwhile, rinse the scallops under cold running water. Cut the larger scallops in half. Put all the scallops in a bowl and sprinkle them with some black pepper. Stir in the lime juice and set the bowl aside.

Put the grilled peppers in a bowl and cover it with plastic film for 1 to 2 minutes (the trapped steam will loosen their skins). Working over the bowl to catch their juices, peel the peppers from top to bottom, then seed them. Coarsely chop the peppers and put them in a food processor or blender along with their reserved juices, the vinegar, thyme and some pepper; purée the mixture.

Pour the oil into a large, heavy frying pan over medium-high heat. When the oil is hot, add the mushrooms and sauté them for 3 minutes, stirring once. Sprinkle the mushrooms with ⅛ teaspoon of the salt, then pour in the wine. Continue cooking the mixture, stirring occasionally, until almost all of the liquid has evaporated — 3 to 5 minutes.

Pour the red pepper purée into the frying pan. Place the scallops on top and sprinkle them with some more black pepper and the remaining salt. Cook the mixture for 1 minute, stirring frequently. Add the spring onions and chicory and continue cooking, stirring frequently, until the scallops are firm — 2 to 3 minutes more. Serve immediately.

SUGGESTED ACCOMPANIMENT: *steamed rice.*

Clams with Orzo

Serves 4 as a main course, 6 as a first course
Working (and total) time: about 25 minutes

Calories **200**
Protein **12g**
Cholesterol **35mg**
Total fat **5g**
Saturated fat **1g**
Sodium **55mg**

36	*littleneck clams, scrubbed*	36
100 g	*orzo (rice-shaped pasta)*	3½ oz
1 tbsp	*virgin olive oil*	1 tbsp
4	*shallots, finely chopped*	4
⅛ tsp	*ground cinnamon*	⅛ tsp
⅛ tsp	*cayenne pepper*	⅛ tsp
1	*ripe tomato, skinned, seeded and chopped*	1
4 tbsp	*chopped fresh parsley*	4 tbsp

Tap the clams and discard any that will not close. Put the clams into a deep pan and pour ¼ litre (8 fl oz) of water over them. Tightly cover the pan and set it over high heat. Steam the clams for 5 to 8 minutes, periodically transferring the opened ones to a bowl. Discard any clams that remain closed.

Remove the clams from their shells and rinse them one by one in the cooking liquid in the pan to dislodge any clinging sand. Set the clams aside, and carefully pour the cooking liquid through a fine strainer into a medium saucepan, leaving behind as much sand as possible. Pour in 2 litres (3½ pints) of water and bring the liquid to the boil. Stir in the orzo and cook it until it is *al dente* — 5 to 10 minutes.

While the orzo is cooking, heat the oil in a large, heavy frying pan over medium heat. Add the shallots and cook them until they are translucent — about 4 minutes. Sprinkle in the cinnamon and cayenne pepper, and cook the mixture for 30 seconds. Add the tomato and parsley and cook the mixture for 1 minute more.

Drain the cooked orzo and stir it and the clams into the shallot-tomato mixture. Cook until the clams are heated through — 1 to 2 minutes.

Serve the clams and orzo in clam or scallop shells, in individual serving dishes or on a platter.

SUGGESTED ACCOMPANIMENT: *courgettes sautéed with celery and thyme.*

Clams and Rice Yucatan-Style

Serves 4
Working time: about 30 minutes
Total time: about 1 hour

Calories **470**
Protein **16g**
Cholesterol **35mg**
Total fat **8g**
Saturated fat **1g**
Sodium **200mg**

36	*clams, scrubbed*	*36*
3	*ripe tomatoes, skinned, seeded and coarsely chopped*	*3*
1	*large onion, coarsely chopped*	*1*
3	*garlic cloves, coarsely chopped*	*3*
3	*fresh hot green chili peppers, seeded and coarsely chopped (caution, page 45)*	*3*
55 cl	*fish stock (recipe, page 136) or water*	*18 fl oz*
2 tbsp	*safflower oil*	*2 tbsp*
275 g	*long-grain rice*	*9 oz*
¼ tsp	*salt*	*¼ tsp*
	freshly ground black pepper	
75 g	*shelled peas, blanched for 1 minute if fresh*	*2½ oz*
1	*lime, juice only*	*1*
	several fresh coriander sprigs	

Purée the tomatoes, onion, garlic, chilies and 12.5 cl (4 fl oz) of the fish stock or water in a food processor or blender. Preheat the oven to 200°C (400°F or Mark 6).

Heat the oil in a large shallow fireproof casserole over medium heat. Add the rice and sauté it in the oil, stirring constantly, until it is lightly browned — 3 to 4 minutes. Stir in the puréed tomato, the remaining stock or water, the salt and black pepper. Bring the mixture to a simmer, reduce the heat to medium low and cook the rice, covered, until most of the liquid has been absorbed — about 15 minutes. Stir in the peas.

Tap the clams and discard any that do not close. Arrange them on top of the rice, cover with foil and bake them until they open — about 10 minutes. Dribble the lime juice over the clams and garnish the dish with the coriander sprigs. Serve immediately.

SUGGESTED ACCOMPANIMENTS: *warm tortillas; chicory and orange salad or chopped avocado salad.*

The sauces that follow are designed to accompany oysters on the half shell; they may be presented alone or in concert. To avoid the risk of eating contaminated shellfish, be sure to purchase the oysters from a reliable fishmonger.

Red Wine Sauce

Serves 4
Working time: about 15 minutes
Total time: about 1 hour and 15 minutes

Calories **265**
Protein **14g**
Cholesterol **95mg**
Total fat **4g**
Saturated fat **1g**
Sodium **265mg**

24	*oysters, shucked (opposite page)*	*24*
¾ litre	*red wine*	*1 ¼ pints*
2	*garlic cloves, finely chopped*	*2*
2 tbsp	*chopped shallot*	*2 tbsp*
1 ½ tbsp	*fresh lemon juice*	*1 ½ tbsp*
1 tsp	*fresh thyme, or ¼ tsp dried thyme*	*1 tsp*
2 tsp	*honey*	*2 tsp*
⅛ tsp	*salt*	*⅛ tsp*
	freshly ground black pepper	

Pour the wine into a non-reactive saucepan over medium heat. Cook the wine until it is reduced to ¼ litre (8 fl oz) — about 20 minutes. Add the garlic, shallot, lemon juice, thyme, honey, salt and pepper, and cook for 10 minutes. Refrigerate the sauce for at least 45 minutes.

Herbed Yogurt Sauce

Serves 4
Working (and total) time: about 30 minutes

Calories **255**
Protein **17g**
Cholesterol **130mg**
Total fat **15g**
Saturated fat **2g**
Sodium **310mg**

24	*oysters, shucked (opposite page)*	*24*
½	*egg yolk*	*½*
1	*egg white*	*1*
2 tbsp	*safflower oil*	*2 tbsp*
1 tbsp	*virgin olive oil*	*1 tbsp*
12.5 cl	*plain low-fat yogurt*	*4 fl oz*
2	*spring onions, trimmed and finely chopped*	*2*
2	*garlic cloves, very finely chopped*	*2*
1 ½ tbsp	*fresh lime juice*	*1 ½ tbsp*
1 tsp	*Dijon mustard*	*1 tsp*
⅛ tsp	*salt*	*⅛ tsp*
	freshly ground black pepper	
1 tbsp	*finely chopped fresh basil or flat-leaf parsley, or 1 tbsp finely cut fresh dill*	*1 tbsp*

Place the egg yolk and egg white in a large bowl. Whisking vigorously, pour the safflower oil into the bowl in a fine, steady stream. Incorporate the olive oil in the same way. Whisk in the yogurt, spring onions, garlic, lime juice, mustard, salt, some pepper, and the basil, parsley or dill. Refrigerate the sauce for at least 20 minutes to let the flavours meld.

Mignonette Sauce with Celery Seeds

Serves 4
Working (and total) time: about 25 minutes

Calories **110**
Protein **14g**
Cholesterol **95mg**
Total fat **4g**
Saturated fat **1g**
Sodium **195mg**

24	*oysters, shucked (below)*	*24*
17.5 cl	*white wine vinegar*	*6 fl oz*
1	*large shallot, very finely chopped*	*1*
1 tsp	*celery seeds*	*1 tsp*
2 tbsp	*finely chopped celery leaves*	*2 tbsp*
1 tsp	*freshly ground black pepper*	*1 tsp*

In a small bowl, whisk together the vinegar, shallot, celery seeds, celery leaves and pepper. Refrigerate the sauce until serving time.

Shucking an Oyster

1 *OPENING THE SHELLS. Scrub the oyster well. Place it on a work surface with its rounder side down to catch the liquid. Grip the oyster with a towel to protect your hand, leaving the hinged end exposed, and force the tip of an oyster knife or other broad blade into the hinge. Twist the blade to prise the shells apart.*

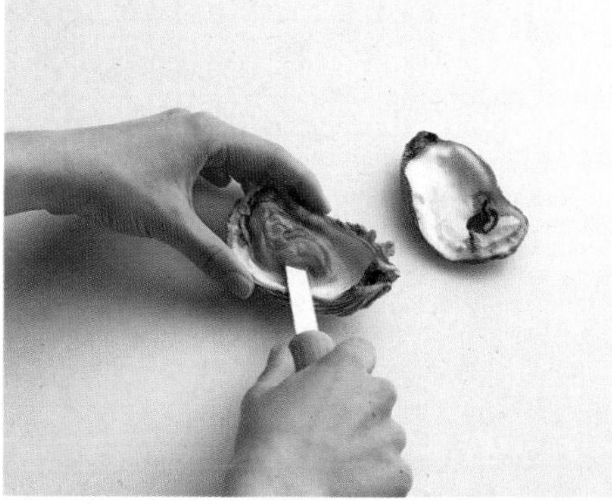

2 *FREEING THE OYSTER. Sliding the knife blade along the inside of the upper shell, sever the muscle that attaches the flesh to the shell. Discard the upper shell, then slide the blade under the oyster and cut it free. Save the rounder shells, if you like, and use them to serve the oysters in.*

Oysters with Julienned Vegetables in Basil-Butter Sauce

Serves 4 as a first course
Working (and total) time: about 30 minutes

Calories **220**
Protein **13g**
Cholesterol **95mg**
Total fat **9g**
Saturated fat **4g**
Sodium **325mg**

20	*large oysters, shucked (page 95) the liquid reserved*	20
3 tbsp	*fresh lemon juice*	3 tbsp
1	*large carrot, peeled and julienned*	1
1	*stick celery, trimmed and julienned*	1
1	*leek, trimmed, split, washed thoroughly to remove all grit, and julienned*	1
12.5 cl	*dry white wine*	4 fl oz
1	*shallot, finely chopped*	1
¼ tsp	*salt*	¼ tsp
	freshly ground black pepper	
2 tbsp	*fresh basil, flat-leaf parsley or coriander, cut into thin strips*	2 tbsp
20 g	*cold unsalted butter*	¾ oz
1	*lemon (optional), cut into wedges*	1

Add 2 tablespoons of the lemon juice to 1 litre (1¾ pints) of water and bring the water to the boil. Drop the carrot julienne into the boiling water; after 30 seconds, add the celery julienne; after 15 seconds more, add the leek julienne. Cook the vegetables for another 15 seconds, then drain and set them aside.

Pour the wine into a large, non-reactive sauté pan. Add the remaining lemon juice and the shallot, and bring the liquid to a simmer. Cook the liquid until it is reduced by half — about 3 minutes — and turn the heat to low. Lay the oysters in the pan in a single layer; pour in the reserved juices and cook the oysters for 30 seconds. Turn the oysters over and cook them until they are heated through — about 30 seconds more. With a slotted spoon, transfer the oysters to warmed plates. Top each oyster with some of the julienned vegetables.

With the pan still set over low heat, add the salt, some pepper and the basil. Whisk in the butter, then ladle some of the sauce over each oyster. Garnish the plates with lemon wedges, if you like, and serve the oysters immediately.

Lobster with Leek and Tomato Compotes

Serves 4
Working time: about 25 minutes
Total time: about 1 hour and 15 minutes

Calories **315**
Protein **30g**
Cholesterol **105mg**
Total fat **3g**
Saturated fat **0g**
Sodium **420mg**

4	*live lobsters (about 600 g/1 ¼ lb each)*	*4*
4	*medium leeks, trimmed, split, washed thoroughly to remove all grit, white parts sliced, green leaves reserved*	*4*
4	*ripe tomatoes, skinned and seeded, skins and seeds reserved, flesh cut into strips about 5 mm (¼ inch) wide*	*4*
1	*tarragon sprig, leaves removed from the stem, both reserved*	*1*
8	*black peppercorns*	*8*
¼ litre	*dry white wine*	*8 fl oz*

Kill two of the lobsters by plunging them into a large pan of boiling water. Tightly cover the pan and boil the lobsters for 1 minute. Remove the lobsters with tongs and repeat the process with the remaining two lobsters. Pour out the water.

Working over the pan to catch the lobsters' juices, use the techniques demonstrated on pages 134-135 to remove the meat and the tomalley from each lobster. Cut the meat into 2.5 cm (1 inch) pieces and reserve it. Put all the shells, legs and tomalley into the pan. Add to the pan the leeks' green leaves, the tomato skins and seeds, the tarragon stem and the black peppercorns. Pour in enough water to cover the shells, and bring the liquid to the boil. Cook the stock for 25 minutes.

Strain the stock into a large, heavy sauté pan, discarding the solids. Boil the stock over high heat until it is reduced by half — about 10 minutes. Add the sliced leeks to the pan and cook them until they are tender — about 3 minutes — then remove them with a slotted spoon and keep them warm. Pour in the wine and boil the liquid for 3 minutes more.

Spoon the lobster meat into the boiling liquid and cook it until it is opaque — about 2 minutes. Remove the lobster meat and keep it warm. Boil the liquid remaining in the pan until it is reduced to ¼ litre (8 fl oz) — about 5 minutes. Add the tomato strips and cook them, stirring gently, until they are heated through — about 2 minutes. Remove the tomato strips and toss them with the tarragon leaves.

Pour the sauce over the lobster and serve it with the leeks and tomatoes.

SUGGESTED ACCOMPANIMENT: *pappardelle, or other wide noodles.*

Lobster in Parsley-Coriander Sauce

Serves 2
Working time: about 30 minutes
Total time: about 40 minutes

Calories **360**
Protein **30g**
Cholesterol **105mg**
Total fat **17g**
Saturated fat **2g**
Sodium **410mg**

2	*live lobsters (about 600 g/1 ¼ lb each)*	*2*
2 tbsp	*virgin olive oil*	*2 tbsp*
125 g	*onion, finely chopped*	*4 oz*
1 tsp	*curry powder*	*1 tsp*
½ tsp	*turmeric*	*½ tsp*
1 tbsp	*fresh lemon juice*	*1 tbsp*
2	*garlic cloves, finely chopped*	*2*
	freshly ground black pepper	
1	*ripe tomato, seeded and finely diced*	*1*
60 g	*fresh parsley, coarsely chopped*	*2 oz*
4 tbsp	*chopped fresh coriander*	*4 tbsp*

Pour enough water into a large pan to fill it about 2.5 cm (1 inch) deep. Bring the water to the boil, place the lobsters in the water and tightly cover the pot. Cook the lobsters until they turn pink — about 10 minutes. Remove the lobsters from the pan. When they are cool enough to handle, extract the meat from the tails and claws as shown on pages 134-135; reserve the shells.

Preheat the oven to 150°C (300°F or Mark 2). Return the lobster shells to the pan and pour in ½ litre (16 fl oz) of water. Bring the water to the boil, reduce the heat to medium and simmer the shells for 10 minutes. Strain the liquid through a fine strainer into a saucepan and reduce it over medium heat until only about ¼ litre (8 fl oz) remains — about 10 minutes.

While the lobster liquid is reducing, cut the tail meat of one of the lobsters into slices about 5 mm (¼ inch) thick. Arrange the slices in an overlapping pattern on an ovenproof serving plate, with the whole claw meat at the top, as illustrated on the right. Slice and arrange the other lobster on another plate in the same way. Cover the plates with foil and put them in the oven.

To prepare the sauce, pour the oil into a large frying pan over medium-high heat. When the oil is hot, add the onion, curry powder and turmeric; cook the mixture, stirring frequently, until the onion is browned — about 5 minutes. Pour in the reduced lobster liquid, lemon juice, garlic and some pepper, and simmer the sauce for 1 minute. Stir in the tomato, parsley and half of the coriander, and remove the pan from the heat.

Remove the lobsters from the oven and lift off the foil. Pour half of the sauce around each lobster. Sprinkle the remaining 2 tablespoons of coriander over the lobsters and serve them immediately.

SUGGESTED ACCOMPANIMENTS: *steamed asparagus and boiled new potatoes.*

Stuffed Lobster

Serves 8
Working time: about 35 minutes
Total time: about 45 minutes

Calories **175**
Protein **16g**
Cholesterol **50mg**
Total fat **5g**
Saturated fat **1g**
Sodium **290mg**

4	*live lobsters (about 600 g/1 ¼ lb each)*	4
6	*slices day-old white bread, crumbled into small pieces*	6
2 tbsp	*virgin olive oil*	2 tbsp
2	*shallots, finely chopped, or 4 tbsp finely chopped onion*	2
4 tbsp	*chopped fresh oregano, marjoram or flat-leaf parsley*	4 tbsp
6	*garlic cloves, finely chopped*	6
	freshly ground black pepper	
6 tbsp	*fresh lemon juice*	6 tbsp
2 tsp	*paprika, preferably Hungarian*	2 tsp

To prepare the stuffing, combine the bread, oil, shallots, half of the oregano, half of the garlic and some pepper in a large bowl. Set the stuffing aside.

In a small bowl, combine the remaining oregano and garlic, the lemon juice, paprika and some pepper. Set the bowl aside.

Preheat the oven to 240°C (475°F or Mark 9).

Kill the lobsters by plunging them into a large pan of boiling water for 1 minute. Remove the lobsters with tongs and let them drain until they are cool enough to handle. Twist off the claws. Using a large, heavy knife, split each lobster down the entire length of the body and tail. Remove the tomalley — and coral, if a female lobster — with a spoon and chop it. Add to the stuffing and mix well. Remove the viscera from the stomach cavity and discard them.

Arrange the lobster halves in a large baking dish with their cut sides up. Gently crack the claws *(page 135)* and arrange them around the tails. Loosely fill the stomach cavities with the stuffing. Dribble the lemon-juice mixture over the tail meat only and place the baking dish in the oven. Bake the lobsters until the stuffing is lightly browned on top — 12 to 15 minutes.

Transfer the split lobsters (not the claws) to a large serving platter and cover them with aluminium foil to keep them warm. Return the claws to the oven and bake them for 5 minutes more. Arrange the claws around the lobsters and serve immediately.

SUGGESTED ACCOMPANIMENT: *cucumber and tomato salad.*

Mussel Risotto

COOKING RICE BY THE REPEATED ADDITION OF LIQUID IS A TECHNIQUE PARTICULAR TO RISOTTO. IT RESULTS IN ESPECIALLY TENDER, MOIST RICE.

Serves 6
Working (and total) time: about 45 minutes

Calories **310**
Protein **20g**
Cholesterol **90mg**
Total fat **9g**
Saturated fat **3g**
Sodium **450mg**

1.5 kg	*mussels, scrubbed and debearded*	*3 lb*
1 tbsp	*safflower oil*	*1 tbsp*
1	*onion, finely chopped*	*1*
185 g	*rice*	*6½ oz*
4 tbsp	*dry white wine*	*4 tbsp*
8 to 10	*saffron threads, crushed (about ⅛ tsp)*	*8 to 10*
90 g	*small broccoli florets*	*3 oz*
15 g	*unsalted butter*	*½ oz*
60 g	*Parmesan cheese, freshly grated*	*2 oz*
¼ tsp	*white pepper*	*¼ tsp*

Put the mussels in a large pan. Pour in 4 tablespoons of water, bring it to the boil, and tightly cover the pan. Steam the mussels until they open — 5 to 6 minutes. With a slotted spoon, transfer the opened mussels to a bowl; discard any that remain closed. Strain the mussel-cooking liquid through a fine strainer into a large measuring jug and set it aside.

Heat the oil in a fireproof casserole over medium heat. Add the onion and cook it, stirring occasionally, until it is translucent — 2 to 3 minutes. Add the rice and stir to coat it with the oil. Cook for 1 minute more. Pour in the wine and cook, stirring, until it has evaporated — about 2 minutes.

Strain into the measuring jug any liquid that has accumulated from the mussels. Add enough water to yield 35 cl (12 fl oz). Pour the liquid into the casserole and stir in the saffron. Bring the liquid to the boil, then reduce the heat to maintain a simmer. Cook the rice, stirring often, until it has absorbed most of the liquid — about 10 minutes.

Stir in ¼ litre (8 fl oz) of hot water and continue to cook the rice, stirring, until the water is absorbed. Pour in another ¼ litre (8 fl oz) of hot water; if necessary to maintain a very moist consistency, pour in an additional 12.5 cl (4 fl oz) of water. The rice is done when it is tender to the bite — 25 to 30 minutes.

While the rice is cooking, remove the mussels from their shells and set the mussels aside; discard the shells. Bring 1 litre (1¾ pints) of water to the boil in a saucepan. Add the broccoli and blanch it until it is barely tender — about 2 minutes. Drain the broccoli and refresh it under cold running water.

Melt the butter in a large, heavy frying pan over medium-high heat. Add the reserved mussels and broccoli florets, and sauté them until they are heated through — 1 to 2 minutes. Stir the cheese and pepper into the cooked rice, then stir in the mussels and broccoli; serve at once.

SUGGESTED ACCOMPANIMENT: *crusty bread.*

Warm Mussel and Potato Salad

Serves 6
Working time: about 30 minutes
Total time: about 40 minutes

Calories **260**
Protein **18g**
Cholesterol **75mg**
Total fat **8g**
Saturated fat **1g**
Sodium **440mg**

1.5 kg	*mussels, scrubbed and debearded*	*3 lb*
1 tbsp	*virgin olive oil*	*1 tbsp*
4	*shallots, finely chopped*	*4*
1	*garlic clove, finely chopped*	*1*
1	*strip orange rind*	*1*
¼ tsp	*ground cumin*	*¼ tsp*
12.5 cl	*dry white wine*	*4 fl oz*
500 g	*waxy potatoes, peeled*	*1 lb*
¼ tsp	*salt*	*¼ tsp*
350 g	*radicchio or red-leaf lettuce*	*12 oz*
1 tbsp	*cut chives*	*1 tbsp*
	Chive-orange dressing	
4 tbsp	*fresh orange juice*	*4 tbsp*
1 tbsp	*sherry vinegar or white wine vinegar*	*1 tbsp*
½ tsp	*ground cumin*	*½ tsp*
1 tbsp	*virgin olive oil*	*1 tbsp*
¼ litre	*plain low-fat yogurt*	*8 fl oz*
2 tbsp	*finely cut chives*	*2 tbsp*
	freshly ground black pepper	

In a large, deep fireproof casserole, heat the olive oil over medium heat. Stir in the shallots, garlic, orange rind and cumin. Reduce the heat to low and cook the mixture, stirring occasionally, until the shallots are soft — 5 to 7 minutes.

Pour in the wine and bring the liquid to the boil. Add the mussels, reduce heat to medium, and cover. Cook the mussels until their shells have opened — 5 to 6 minutes. Discard any that remain closed. Pour off the cooking liquid and set the mussels aside to cool.

While the mussels are cooking, put the potatoes in a saucepan, cover them with cold water, and sprinkle in

the salt. Bring to the boil, and cook the potatoes until tender — about 20 minutes. Drain and set aside.

To prepare the dressing, combine the orange juice, vinegar and cumin in a bowl. Slowly whisk in the oil, the yogurt, the 2 tablespoons of chives and a generous grinding of pepper.

Remove the mussels from their shells and transfer them to a clean bowl; add half of the dressing and toss well. Cut the potatoes into slices about 1 cm (½ inch) thick; toss the slices with the remaining dressing.

Lay the radicchio or lettuce round the edge of a large platter or individual plates. Arrange the potatoes in an overlapping ring just inside the lettuce, then spoon the mussels into the centre. Sprinkle the dish with the tablespoon of cut chives and serve.

Preparing Molluscs for Cooking: To Purge or Not to Purge?

The notion of purging clams and mussels seems guaranteed to incite debate among cooks. Some feel that it is an essential first step, for it rids the shellfish of the sand they ingest while feeding and burrowing. Others maintain that the process rids them of flavour as well.

If you elect to purge molluscs, first scrub all debris from the outsides of their shells. Then place them in a bucket or the kitchen sink and cover them with about 5 cm (2 inches) of cool water. Sprinkle 60 g (2 oz) of cornmeal into the water and let the clams or mussels stand for up to 30 minutes; the molluscs will take up the cornmeal and expel the sand or grit.

Mussels with Green and Yellow Peppers

Serves 4 as a first course
Working time: about 20 minutes
Total time: about 50 minutes

Calories **110**
Protein **6g**
Cholesterol **25mg**
Total fat **8g**
Saturated fat **1g**
Sodium **255mg**

24	*large mussels, scrubbed and debearded*	24
½	*sweet green pepper, seeded, deribbed and diced*	½
½	*sweet yellow pepper, seeded, deribbed and diced*	½
1	*small ripe tomato, skinned, seeded and finely chopped*	1
1	*garlic clove, finely chopped*	1
1 tbsp	*finely chopped shallot*	1 tbsp
1 tbsp	*balsamic vinegar or red wine vinegar*	1 tbsp
2 tbsp	*safflower oil*	2 tbsp
⅛ tsp	*salt*	⅛ tsp
	freshly ground black pepper	
8	*drops Tabasco sauce*	8

Pour 4 tablespoons of water into a large pan. Add the mussels, cover the pan and bring the water to the boil. Steam the mussels until their shells open — 4 to 5 minutes. Transfer the opened mussels to a shallow dish. Discard any mussels that remain closed.

Working over the dish to catch the juices, remove the top shell from each mussel and discard it. Using a spoon, scoop beneath the mussel to sever the connective tissue that attaches the mussel to the bottom shell. Return the mussel to the shell and transfer it to a serving platter. Strain the collected mussel liquid through a fine strainer into a cup and set it aside.

Combine the peppers, tomato, garlic, shallot and vinegar in a small, non-reactive saucepan. Let the mixture stand for 5 minutes, then whisk in the oil, 1 tablespoon of the strained mussel liquid, the salt, some pepper and the Tabasco sauce. Bring to a simmer over medium heat and cook for 30 seconds. Immediately spoon some of the mixture on to each mussel. Refrigerate, covered, for at least 30 minutes; serve cold.

Prawn and French Bean Salad

Serves 4
Working time: about 30 minutes
Total time: about 1 hour

Calories **185**
Protein **20g**
Cholesterol **135mg**
Total fat **6g**
Saturated fat **1g**
Sodium **235mg**

500 g	*prawns, shells left on*	*1 lb*
750 g	*French beans, trimmed and cut in half*	*1½ lb*
1½ tbsp	*tarragon vinegar*	*1½ tbsp*
1 tbsp	*safflower oil*	*1 tbsp*
2 tbsp	*chopped fresh tarragon, or 2 tsp dried tarragon*	*2 tbsp*
2 tbsp	*finely cut chives*	*2 tbsp*
¼ tsp	*salt*	*¼ tsp*
	freshly ground black pepper	
12.5 cl	*plain low-fat yogurt*	*4 fl oz*
1 tbsp	*soured cream*	*1 tbsp*
1½ tsp	*Dijon mustard*	*1½ tsp*
1 tsp	*tomato paste*	*1 tsp*
1 tbsp	*chopped fresh parsley*	*1 tbsp*

Bring 2 litres (3½ pints) of water to the boil in a large saucepan. Add the beans and boil them until they are just tender — about 6 minutes. Drain the beans and refresh them under cold running water. Pat the beans dry and transfer them to a bowl. Set the bowl aside.

If the prawns are raw, bring 1 litre (1¾ pints) of water to a simmer in the saucepan. Add the prawns, cover the pan, and simmer the prawns until they are opaque — 2 to 3 minutes. Drain them and let them cool enough to handle. Peel the prawns (and, if you like, devein them). Add the the prawns to the beans.

In a small bowl, whisk together the vinegar, oil, half of the tarragon, 1 tablespoon of the chives, ⅛ teaspoon of the salt and some pepper. Arrange the prawns and beans on a serving platter and spoon the vinegar-and-oil marinade over it. Let the dish marinate at room temperature for 30 minutes.

Near the end of the marinating time, prepare the dressing: whisk together the yogurt, soured cream, mustard and tomato paste. Stir in the parsley, the remaining tarragon and the remaining chives, the remaining salt and some pepper. Pour the dressing into a small serving bowl and serve it with the salad.

SUGGESTED ACCOMPANIMENT: *wholemeal pitta.*

Sautéed Prawns with Sherry and Chilies

Serves 4
Working time: about 20 minutes
Total time: about 1 hour

Calories **140**
Protein **16g**
Cholesterol **140mg**
Total fat **4g**
Saturated fat **1g**
Sodium **55mg**

500 g	*raw Mediterranean prawns, peeled and deveined if necessary, shells reserved*	*1 lb*
1	*whole garlic bulb, cloves separated and peeled*	*1*
4	*dried red chili peppers (caution, page 45)*	*4*
1 tsp	*fresh rosemary, or ½ tsp dried rosemary*	*1 tsp*
½ tsp	*fennel seeds*	*½ tsp*
6 tbsp	*dry sherry*	*6 tbsp*
1	*sweet red pepper, seeded, deribbed and julienned*	*1*
1	*spring onion, trimmed and julienned*	*1*
15 g	*unsalted butter*	*½ oz*

Put the prawn shells in a saucepan with the garlic, chili peppers, rosemary, fennel seeds and 1 litre (1¾ pints) of water. Bring the water to the boil, then reduce the heat to medium low and simmer for 30 minutes.

Strain the poaching liquid, discard the solids and return the liquid to the pan. Boil rapidly until only about 35 cl (12 fl oz) remains — 5 to 10 minutes. Pour in the sherry and bring to a simmer. Poach the prawns until they are opaque — approximately 1 minute. Remove them with a slotted spoon and set them aside.

Boil the remaining liquid until only 2 to 3 tablespoons remain — about 5 minutes. Add the julienned red pepper, reduce the heat to medium, and cook for 2 minutes. Return the prawns to the pan. Add the spring onion and butter, and stir until the butter has melted and the prawns are warm. Serve immediately.

SUGGESTED ACCOMPANIMENT: *steamed rice.*

EDITOR'S NOTE: *Served cold, this dish makes an ideal prelude to summer meals; oil should be used in place of butter. Cooked prawns may be used; they do not require poaching.*

Seven-Spice Stew with Mussels, Squid and Prawns

Serves 6
Working (and total) time: about 1 hour

Calories **165**
Protein **17g**
Cholesterol **130mg**
Total fat **2g**
Saturated fat **0g**
Sodium **265mg**

750 g	*mussels, scrubbed and debearded*	*1½ lb*
250 g	*squid, cleaned and skinned (page 132)*	*8 oz*
250 g	*large raw prawns, peeled and deveined if necessary*	*8 oz*
1	*onion, chopped*	*1*
¼ litre	*dry white wine*	*8 fl oz*
2	*ripe tomatoes, skinned, seeded and chopped*	*2*
1	*whole garlic bulb, cloves peeled and thinly sliced*	*1*
¼ tsp	*each ground turmeric, cumin, coriander*	*¼ tsp*
⅛ tsp	*each ground allspice, cloves, cardamom*	*⅛ tsp*
⅛ tsp	*cayenne pepper*	*⅛ tsp*

Put the mussels in a deep pan, together with the onion and the wine. Cover the pan tightly and cook the mussels over medium-high heat until they open — about 5 minutes. Discard any mussels that remain closed. Let the mussels cool, then remove them from their shells and set them aside. Strain the mussel-cooking liquid into a bowl and let it stand for 2 to 3 minutes to allow any sand to settle out. Slowly pour most of the liquid into a large, heavy frying pan, leaving the sand behind.

Add the tomatoes, garlic and spices to the frying pan. Bring the liquid to the boil, then reduce the heat to medium low and simmer the mixture until the garlic is tender — about 5 minutes.

Meanwhile, prepare the squid. Slit the pouches up one side and lay them flat on the work surface. Use a sharp knife to score a criss-cross pattern on the inside of each pouch. Cut the scored pouches into 4 cm (1½ inch) squares. Chop the tentacles into small pieces.

Add the squid to the liquid simmering in the frying pan. Cover the pan and cook the mixture until the squid pieces have curled up — about 1 minute. Add the prawns, cover the pan and continue cooking until the prawns are opaque — approximately 1 minute more. Finally, add the mussels and cook the stew for 1 minute to heat the mussels through. Serve at once.

SUGGESTED ACCOMPANIMENT: *couscous with raisins and almonds.*

EDITOR'S NOTE: Cooked prawns can be used instead of the raw ones; add them with the mussels at the end.

Grilled Prawns with Tomato-Ginger Sauce

Serves 4
Working time: about 40 minutes
Total time: about 1 hour and 15 minutes

Calories **215**
Protein **17g**
Cholesterol **130mg**
Total fat **8g**
Saturated fat **1g**
Sodium **70mg**

24	*large raw prawns (about 500 g/1 lb), peeled and deveined*	*24*
1	*onion, chopped*	*1*
12.5 cl	*dry white wine*	*4 fl oz*
2 tbsp	*fresh lemon juice*	*2 tbsp*
1 tbsp	*virgin olive oil*	*1 tbsp*
	Tomato-ginger sauce	
1 tbsp	*virgin olive oil*	*1 tbsp*
3	*spring onions, trimmed and chopped*	*3*
6	*garlic cloves, chopped*	*6*
1 tbsp	*finely chopped fresh ginger root*	*1 tbsp*
2	*fresh hot green chili peppers, seeded and chopped (caution, page 45)*	*2*
¼ tsp	*ground coriander*	*¼ tsp*
¼ tsp	*ground cumin*	*¼ tsp*
¼ tsp	*dry mustard*	*¼ tsp*
3	*ripe tomatoes, skinned, seeded and chopped*	*3*
1 tsp	*brown sugar*	*1 tsp*
1 tbsp	*red wine vinegar*	*1 tbsp*

In a bowl, combine the onion, wine, lemon juice and oil. Add the prawns and let them marinate in the refrigerator for 1 hour.

Meanwhile, make the sauce. Pour the oil into a large, heavy frying pan over medium-high heat. When the oil is hot, add the spring onions, garlic, ginger and chili peppers; cook for 2 minutes, stirring constantly. Stir in the coriander, cumin and mustard, and cook the mixture for 1 minute more. Add the tomatoes and cook them, stirring constantly, for 1 minute. Remove the pan from the heat and stir in the brown sugar and vinegar. Transfer the sauce to a serving bowl and let it cool.

Near the end of the marinating time, preheat the grill. Thread the prawns in interlocking pairs on to four skewers. Brush the prawns with any remaining marinade and grill them about 5 cm (2 inches) below the heat source until they are opaque — approximately 3 minutes.

Serve the prawns on their skewers atop a bed of rice, with the sauce presented alongside.

SUGGESTED ACCOMPANIMENTS: *steamed rice; endive salad.*

Broccoli-Studded Prawns

Serves 4
Working (and total) time: about 30 minutes

Calories **160**
Protein **17g**
Cholesterol **130mg**
Total fat **8g**
Saturated fat **1g**
Sodium **155mg**

24	*Mediterranean prawns (about 600 g/1¼ lb), peeled, tails left on*	24
24	*broccoli florets, each stem trimmed to 2.5 cm (1 inch) long and tapered to a point, blanched for 1 minute*	24
2	*spring onions, trimmed and chopped*	2
1	*garlic clove, finely chopped*	1
2 tsp	*finely chopped fresh ginger root*	2 tsp
2 tbsp	*rice vinegar*	2 tbsp
2 tbsp	*rice wine or dry sherry*	2 tbsp
1 tsp	*chili paste with garlic*	1 tsp
1 tsp	*tomato paste*	1 tsp
1 tsp	*cornflour, mixed with 2 tbsp water*	1 tsp
2 tbsp	*safflower oil*	2 tbsp

Using a skewer, make a 5 mm (¼ inch) diameter hole through each prawn from front to back, about one third of the way from its larger end. Insert a broccoli stem into the hole so that the floret nestles within the curve of the prawn, as shown. Transfer the prawns to a bowl with the spring onions, garlic and ginger; toss the mixture gently and let it stand for 10 minutes.

While the prawns are marinating, combine the vinegar, rice wine or sherry, chili paste, tomato paste and the cornflour mixture in a small bowl. Set aside.

Heat the oil in a wok or heavy frying pan over medium-high heat. Add half the prawns and gently stir-fry them until they are opaque and firm —about 2 minutes. Remove and keep warm. Stir-fry the second batch. Return the first batch to the wok and pour in the sauce. Stirring gently to coat the prawns, cook until the sauce thickens — about 1 minute.

SUGGESTED ACCOMPANIMENT: *rice with sweet peppers and spring onions.*

Gingered Prawns on Black Beans

Serves 6
Working time: about 1 hour
Total time: about 9 hours

Calories **425**
Protein **30g**
Cholesterol **110mg**
Total fat **6g**
Saturated fat **1g**
Sodium **345mg**

600 g	*large raw prawns, peeled and deveined, the shells reserved*	1¼ lb
2.5 cm	*piece of fresh ginger root, peeled and thinly sliced, plus 1 tbsp chopped fresh ginger root*	1 inch
35 cl	*dry white wine*	12 fl oz
500 g	*dried black beans, soaked for at least 8 hours and drained*	1 lb
2	*onions, chopped*	2
4	*garlic cloves, 2 crushed and 2 very thinly sliced*	4
1	*cinnamon stick, broken into 3 or 4 pieces*	1
	freshly ground black pepper	
¼ tsp	*salt*	¼ tsp
1 tbsp	*grated lemon rind*	1 tbsp
2 tbsp	*virgin olive oil*	2 tbsp
½ tsp	*ground cinnamon*	½ tsp
1 tsp	*fresh lemon juice*	1 tsp
3	*spring onions, trimmed and thinly sliced*	3

Put the prawn shells in a large saucepan. Add the ginger slices, ¼ litre (8 fl oz) of the wine and ½ litre (16 fl oz) of water, and bring the mixture to the boil. Reduce the heat to medium and cook until the liquid is reduced by half — about 30 minutes. Strain the stock into a bowl, pressing down on the shells to extract any liquid, and set the bowl aside.

While the shells are cooking, put the drained beans in a large, heavy-bottomed saucepan along with the onions, crushed garlic cloves, the pieces of cinnamon stick and some pepper. Pour in enough water to cover the beans by about 4 cm (1½ inches) and boil the beans for 10 minutes. Skim off the foam and reduce the heat to low. Add the prawn stock, salt and lemon rind, and simmer the mixture until the beans are tender but not mushy and a thick sauce results — 1½ to 2 hours. Remove the cinnamon-stick pieces and discard them.

About 5 minutes before the beans finish cooking, pour the oil into a large, heavy frying pan over medium-high heat. When the oil is hot, add the prawns and sprinkle them with some pepper. Add the chopped ginger, the thinly sliced garlic and the ground cinnamon, and sauté the prawns, stirring frequently, for 3 minutes. Pour the lemon juice and the remaining wine into the pan; continue cooking the mixture, stirring frequently, until the prawns are opaque and the liquid is reduced to a glaze — 2 to 3 minutes more. Stir in the spring onions.

Pour the beans on to a serving platter and top them with the prawn mixture. Serve immediately.

SUGGESTED ACCOMPANIMENT: *crisp green salad.*

Squid Stewed in Red Wine

Serves 4
Working time: about 20 minutes
Total time: about 1 hour and 30 minutes

Calories **355**
Protein **21g**
Cholesterol **265mg**
Total fat **9g**
Saturated fat **1g**
Sodium **480mg**

750 g	*squid, cleaned and skinned (page 132)*	*1½ lb*
2 tbsp	*virgin olive oil*	*2 tbsp*
¼ tsp	*salt*	*¼ tsp*
3	*medium leeks, trimmed, split, washed thoroughly to remove all traces of grit, and chopped*	*3*
20	*garlic cloves*	*20*
500 g	*ripe tomatoes, skinned, seeded and chopped, or 400 g (14 oz) canned whole tomatoes, drained and chopped*	*1 lb*
35 cl	*red wine*	*12 fl oz*
250 g	*courgettes, sliced into thin rounds*	*8 oz*
4 tbsp	*basil or flat parsley leaves, cut into thin strips*	*4 tbsp*
	freshly ground black pepper	

Heat ½ tablespoon of the olive oil in a large, heavy frying pan over medium-high heat. Add the squid and sauté it, stirring often, until it is opaque — 2 to 3 minutes. Sprinkle ⅛ teaspoon of the salt on the squid and transfer the squid to a large, heavy-bottomed fireproof casserole.

Reduce the heat under the frying pan to medium low. Pour 1 tablespoon of oil into the pan, then add the leeks and garlic cloves. Cover and cook, shaking the pan occasionally to prevent the leeks and garlic from sticking, until they begin to turn golden-brown — about 10 minutes.

Transfer the leeks and garlic to the casserole containing the squid. Add the tomatoes and wine, and bring the mixture to the boil. Reduce the heat to low, cover the casserole, and simmer the stew until the squid is tender — about 1 hour.

Meanwhile, pour the remaining oil into the frying pan over medium heat. Add the courgettes and cook,

stirring occasionally, until the courgettes are soft but not brown — about 3 minutes. Sprinkle the courgettes with the remaining salt, transfer them to a bowl and set aside.

Before serving the stew, add the softened courgettes, the basil or parsley, and some pepper; stir gently to mix them in, and serve immediately.

SUGGESTED ACCOMPANIMENT: *vermicelli or thin spaghetti tossed with fresh herbs.*
EDITOR'S NOTE: *Octopus can be used instead of the squid.*

Stir-Fried Squid with Asparagus and Mushrooms

Serves 4
Working time: about 35 minutes
Total time: about 45 minutes

Calories **230**
Protein **20g**
Cholesterol **265mg**
Total fat **8g**
Saturated fat **1g**
Sodium **565mg**

750 g	*squid, cleaned (page 1·32)*	*1½ lb*
8	*dried Chinese mushrooms, covered with ¼ litre (8 fl oz) boiling water and soaked for 20 minutes*	*8*
2 tbsp	*rice wine*	*2 tbsp*
2	*garlic cloves, finely chopped*	*2*
2 tbsp	*safflower oil*	*2 tbsp*
250 g	*asparagus, trimmed and sliced diagonally into 4 cm (1½ inch) lengths*	*8 oz*
4	*spring onions, trimmed and thinly sliced diagonally*	*4*
1 tbsp	*low-sodium soy sauce or shoyu*	*1 tbsp*
1 tbsp	*rice vinegar*	*1 tbsp*
1 tbsp	*fermented black beans, rinsed and mashed*	*1 tbsp*
2 tsp	*cornflour*	*2 tsp*

Remove the mushrooms from their soaking liquid and set them aside. Carefully pour the liquid into a small saucepan, leaving behind any grit. Boil the mushroom-soaking liquid until it is reduced to 4 tablespoons — about 5 minutes. Set the pan aside. Meanwhile, stem the mushrooms and slice each one into quarters.

Slit the squid pouches and then flatten them out on a work surface. With a sharp knife, score the inside surface of each pouch in a crosshatch pattern. Cut the pouches into 2.5 cm (1 inch) squares. Combine the squares and the tentacles with the rice wine and the garlic. Marinate the squid in this mixture for 15 minutes at room temperature.

Drain the squid, reserving the marinade. Heat 1 tablespoon of the safflower oil in a wok or a large, heavy frying pan over high heat. Add half of the squid pieces and stir-fry them until the squares are tightly curled — about 2 minutes. Remove and set aside. Heat ½ tablespoon of the oil in the wok or pan and stir-fry the second batch of squid; set it aside with the first.

Heat the remaining oil in the wok or pan. Add the mushrooms, asparagus and spring onions, and stir-fry them for 2 minutes. Add the soy sauce, vinegar, fermented black beans and the reserved marinade, and cook the mixture for 1 minute longer.

Combine the reduced mushroom-soaking liquid and the cornflour, and pour the mixture into the wok or pan. Stir the vegetables until the sauce has thickened. Combine the squid with the vegetables and stir a few times to heat the squid through. Serve at once.

SUGGESTED ACCOMPANIMENT: *Chinese noodles or brown rice.*
EDITOR'S NOTE: *Octopus can be used instead of the squid.*

4 *Cooked in minutes, mussels, scallops, prawns and crab claws are served in a broth seasoned with saffron, fennel seeds and thyme (recipe, opposite).*

Microwaving Fish and Shellfish

Freshness of flavour, high nutritional value, speedy preparation — these beneficent basics of fish and shellfish cookery get an extra boost from the microwave oven. Furthermore, even the leanest specimens retain their moisture. Since the addition of extra liquid is seldom needed, no vitamins or minerals are lost in the cooking medium.

Fish steaks and fillets make the best candidates for microwaving; their uniform texture and shape allow them to cook evenly. For best results, place the thicker portions towards the outside of the dish or overlap the thinner sections in a wreath-like fashion. Then cover the dish with plastic film and set the oven on high power. The results are similar to conventional steaming or poaching.

Shellfish also cook to advantage in the microwave oven. Prawns, scallops, oysters and clams need only 2 to 3 minutes per 500 g (1 lb); however, they should be stirred half way through the process. A whole lobster steams in 8 to 10 minutes. Whole crabs, on the other hand, cook unevenly because of their shape and numerous appendages; crab meat out of the shell presents no problem.

The microwave oven even offers an easy way to open stubborn clams or oysters. Simply arrange the molluscs in a dish with their hinges facing out and cover them. Microwave on high power until the shells have opened just slightly.

The 16 recipes in this chapter have been tested in 625-watt and 700-watt ovens; the term "high" is used to indicate full power. To avoid overcooking, check fish and shellfish for doneness after the shortest time specified. Remember that food continues to cook briefly after it has left the microwave. Fish should still be slightly translucent in the centre when removed from the oven. Set the dish aside for 3 to 5 minutes, and it will be done to a perfect turn.

Shellfish Cioppino

THIS RECIPE IS A FRESH ADAPTATION OF THE TRADITIONAL CIOPPINO, A FISH STEW INTRODUCED BY ITALIAN SETTLERS IN CALIFORNIA.

Serves 4
Working time: about 20 minutes
Total time: about 50 minutes

Calories **210**
Protein **21g**
Cholesterol **90mg**
Total fat **5g**
Saturated fat **2g**
Sodium **340mg**

4	*large crab claws*	4
12	*mussels, scrubbed and debearded*	12
250 g	*shelled scallops, bright white connective tissue removed, scallops rinsed and patted dry*	8 oz
8	*large prawns (about 125 g/¼ lb), peeled (the tails left on) and deveined*	8
15 g	*unsalted butter*	½ oz
2	*garlic cloves, finely chopped*	2
1	*medium leek, trimmed, split, washed thoroughly to remove any grit, and chopped*	1
1	*ripe tomato, skinned, seeded and chopped*	1
½ litre	*fish stock (recipe, page 136)*	16 fl oz
¼ litre	*dry vermouth*	8 fl oz
10	*saffron threads, crushed*	10
¼ tsp	*fennel seeds*	¼ tsp
½ tsp	*fresh thyme, or ¼ tsp dried thyme*	½ tsp
¼ tsp	*salt*	¼ tsp
	freshly ground black pepper	

Put the butter in a bowl, cover it with plastic film or a lid, and microwave it on high until the butter is melted — 40 seconds. Add the garlic and the leek, and stir to coat them with the butter. Cover the bowl again and cook the mixture on medium high (70 per cent power) for 2 minutes, stirring once half way through the cooking time.

Add the tomato, stock, vermouth, saffron, fennel seeds, thyme, salt and some pepper; then cover, leaving a slight opening to let steam escape, and microwave on high for 7 minutes. Uncover, and cook until it is reduced by one third — about 15 minutes more.

While the stock mixture is cooking, twist each crab claw at the first joint to break off the pincer segment. With a nutcracker, crack each pincer segment across its thickest part *(page 133)*. Remove the part of the ▶

shell between the crack and the open end of the segment, leaving the claw meat in place; this makes the meat easier to remove at the table. Crack the other claw segments, remove and reserve the meat, and discard the shells.

When the stock mixture is sufficiently reduced, remove it from the oven and set it aside. Put the mussels in a bowl and cover the bowl with plastic film or a lid. Microwave the mussels on high until they begin to open — about 2 minutes. Remove the mussels that have opened and set them aside in their shells; discard any mussels that remain closed.

Put the reserved crab meat, the crab claws, the scallops and prawns in the bowl with the stock mixture. Cover the bowl, leaving a slight opening to allow steam to escape, and microwave the shellfish on high for 2 minutes. Stir the shellfish to rearrange them, then add the mussels, spooning some of the liquid over them. Cook the stew on high until all the shellfish are cooked through — about 90 seconds more. Serve the cioppino piping hot.

SUGGESTED ACCOMPANIMENT: *salad of cos lettuce leaves and radishes.*

Orange-Ginger Trout

Serves 8
Working time: about 30 minutes
Total time: about 1 hour

Calories **250**
Protein **28g**
Cholesterol **85mg**
Total fat **10g**
Saturated fat **2g**
Sodium **155mg**

4	*trout, about 500 g (1 lb) each, filleted and skinned (page 130)*	4
2	*oranges, the grated rind and juice of 1 reserved, the other left whole*	2
1 tbsp	*finely chopped fresh ginger root*	1 tbsp
2	*shallots, finely chopped*	2
¼ litre	*dry white wine*	8 fl oz
1 kg	*spinach, washed and stemmed*	2 lb
1	*garlic clove, finely chopped*	1
¼ tsp	*salt*	¼ tsp
	freshly ground black pepper	
15 g	*unsalted butter*	½ oz

Rinse the fillets under cold running water and pat them dry with paper towels. In a 20 cm (8 inch) round baking dish, combine the grated orange rind, orange juice, ginger, shallots and wine. Place the fillets in the liquid and let them marinate at room temperature for 30 minutes.

Put half of the spinach, with the water still clinging to it, and half of the garlic in a bowl and microwave them on high for 3 minutes. Repeat the process to cook the remaining spinach and garlic; set both of the batches aside.

Meanwhile, peel and section the whole orange, and remove the outer membrane from each segment.

Remove the fillets from their marinade. Fold each fillet loosely in thirds, with the boned side out and the ends tucked under the middle, envelope-fashion. Add the salt and some pepper to the marinade and stir it well. Replace the folded fillets in the marinade, with their sides not touching, and microwave them on high until they are slightly translucent — 5 to 7 minutes. Remove the fillets from the cooking liquid and set them aside.

Strain the liquid into a small bowl and microwave it on high, uncovered, until it is reduced by half — about

5 minutes. Add the butter and cook the mixture for 2 minutes more.

Arrange the spinach in an even layer in the baking dish. Place the folded fillets on the spinach bed and top each one with an orange segment. Return the dish to the oven and microwave it on high until it is warmed through — about 90 seconds. Pour the sauce over all and serve immediately.

SUGGESTED ACCOMPANIMENT: *lettuce and tomato salad.*

Scallop and Prawn Brochettes

Serves 4
Working (and total) time: about 15 minutes

Calories **95**
Protein **17g**
Cholesterol **75mg**
Total fat **1g**
Saturated fat **0g**
Sodium **230mg**

250 g	*shelled scallops, bright white connective tissue removed, scallops rinsed and halved horizontally*	*8 oz*
250 g	*raw Mediterranean prawns, peeled and deveined*	*8 oz*
1 tbsp	*low-sodium soy sauce or shoyu*	*1 tbsp*
1	*lime, juice only*	*1*
½ tsp	*honey*	*½ tsp*

Combine the soy sauce, lime juice and honey in a small bowl. Thread the scallops and prawns on to wooden skewers (do not use metal). Brush the brochettes with half of the sauce.

Set the brochettes on a microwave roasting rack or in a baking dish and cook them on high for 4 minutes, turning them over mid-way through the cooking. Brush the brochettes with the remaining sauce and serve them at once.

SUGGESTED ACCOMPANIMENT: *spaghetti squash tossed with diced sweet red pepper and dark sesame oil, or steamed vegetable marrow.*

Hake Timbales with Tomato-Chili Sauce

Serves 8 as a first course
Working (and total) time: about 45 minutes

Calories **110**
Protein **12g**
Cholesterol **20mg**
Total fat **3g**
Saturated fat **1g**
Sodium **170mg**

500 g	*hake fillets (or cod), rinsed, patted dry and finely chopped*	*1 lb*
2	*onions, finely chopped*	*2*
2	*fresh hot green chili peppers, seeded and finely chopped (caution, page 45)*	*2*
2 tsp	*finely chopped lime rind*	*2 tsp*
1 tbsp	*chopped fresh oregano, or ½ tsp dried oregano*	*1 tbsp*
1 tbsp	*virgin olive oil*	*1 tbsp*
20 g	*fresh breadcrumbs*	*¾ oz*
12.5 cl	*skimmed milk*	*4 fl oz*
12.5 cl	*plain low-fat yogurt*	*4 fl oz*
2	*egg whites*	*2*
⅛ tsp	*salt*	*⅛ tsp*
8	*oregano or parsley sprigs (optional)*	*8*
	Tomato-chili sauce	
3	*ripe tomatoes, skinned, seeded and chopped or 400 g (14 oz) canned whole tomatoes, drained and chopped*	*3*
2	*fresh hot green chili peppers, seeded and finely chopped (caution, page 45)*	*2*
1 tbsp	*chopped fresh oregano, or ½ tsp dried oregano*	*1 tbsp*
1 tsp	*red wine vinegar*	*1 tsp*
⅛ tsp	*salt*	*⅛ tsp*

In a small bowl, stir together the onions, green chili peppers, lime rind, oregano and oil. Cover the bowl with plastic film or a lid and microwave it on high for 4 minutes, stirring the mixture half way through the cooking time. Set the bowl aside for 2 minutes.

In a 2 litre (3½ pint) bowl, combine the breadcrumbs, milk and yogurt. Add the fish and the onion mixture; stir well, then add the egg whites and salt. Beat the mixture until it comes away from the sides of the bowl.

Spoon the fish mixture into eight lightly oiled 12.5 cl (4 fl oz) ramekins. Cover each ramekin loosely with plastic film, then microwave them on high for 8 minutes, stopping after 4 minutes to rotate each one a half turn. Remove the timbales from the oven and let them stand while you prepare the sauce.

Combine the sauce ingredients in a bowl and stir well. Turn the timbales out on to plates. Ladle some of the sauce around the timbales and pour the remaining sauce into its own serving bowl. Garnish each plate with the oregano or parsley sprigs if you wish, and serve immediately.

Soused Norway Haddock

SOUSED (PICKLED) FISH CAN BE MADE UP TO 24 HOURS IN ADVANCE AND REFRIGERATED. ITS FLAVOUR IMPROVES WITH TIME.

Serves 8 as a first course
Working time: about 20 minutes
Total time: about 1 hour and 20 minutes

Calories **65**
Protein **11g**
Cholesterol **25mg**
Total fat **2g**
Saturated fat **0g**
Sodium **65mg**

500 g	*Norway haddock fillets (or herring), skin on*	*1 lb*
1	*small onion, sliced, rings separated*	*1*
1	*small carrot, quartered and sliced*	*1*
1	*bay leaf*	*1*
½ tsp	*coriander seeds*	*½ tsp*
¼ tsp	*mustard seeds*	*¼ tsp*
¼ tsp	*celery seeds*	*¼ tsp*
8	*black peppercorns*	*8*
4 tbsp	*cider vinegar*	*4 tbsp*
¼ tsp	*salt*	*¼ tsp*

In a 30 cm (12 inch) round glass dish, combine the onion, carrot, bay leaf, coriander seeds, mustard seeds, celery seeds and peppercorns with ¼ litre (8 fl oz) of water. Cover the dish and microwave it on high for 3 minutes. Rotate the dish half a turn and cook the contents for 2 minutes more. Remove the plate from the oven and let it stand for 3 minutes.

Add the vinegar and salt to the mixture and stir gently to dissolve the salt. Rinse the fillets under cold running water. Place the fillets in the dish, with their skin sides up and their edges not touching. Cook the fish on high, uncovered, for 2 minutes. Turn the plate half a turn and cook until the fish feels firm to the touch — 1 to 2 minutes more. Refrigerate the fish, in its liquid, for at least 1 hour. Serve the soused fish chilled or at room temperature.

SUGGESTED ACCOMPANIMENT: *dark rye bread.*

Salmon Steaks in Three-Pepper Stew

Serves 4
Working time: about 30 minutes
Total time: about 45 minutes

Calories **310**
Protein **25g**
Cholesterol **90mg**
Total fat **18g**
Saturated fat **4g**
Sodium **155mg**

4	*salmon steaks (about 150 g/5 oz each)*	4
1 kg	*ripe tomatoes, skinned, seeded and chopped*	2 lb
2	*sweet red peppers, seeded, deribbed and cut into 5 mm (¼ inch) wide strips*	2
2	*sweet green peppers, seeded, deribbed and cut into 5 mm (¼ inch) wide strips*	2
2	*fresh hot green chili peppers, finely chopped (caution, page 45)*	2
2	*garlic cloves, finely chopped*	2
1 tbsp	*chopped fresh marjoram, or 1 tsp dried marjoram*	1 tbsp
⅛ tsp	*salt*	⅛ tsp
	freshly ground black pepper	
1 tbsp	*virgin olive oil*	1 tbsp
1	*lime, juice only*	1

Put the chopped tomatoes in a fine strainer and set them aside to drain for at least 30 minutes.

While the tomatoes are draining, remove the skin from the salmon steaks with a small, sharp knife. Divide each steak into two boneless pieces by cutting down each side of the backbone and around the ribs. Reassemble each steak as shown in the photograph, with the skinned sides facing out, the thicker parts interlocking, and the tapered flaps wrapped around the whole. Put the steaks in a baking dish, cover it with plastic film and set it aside.

In a second baking dish, combine the red, green and chili peppers with the garlic, marjoram, salt, some black pepper and 1 teaspoon of the oil. Cover the dish tightly and microwave the contents on high for 4 minutes, stirring once mid-way through the cooking time. Remove the pepper stew from the oven and let it stand while you cook the fish.

Microwave the fish on high, rotating the dish half a turn after 2 minutes, until the fish is slightly translucent — about 4 minutes in all. Let the fish stand while you prepare the tomato sauce. Put the drained tomatoes in a small bowl with the lime juice and the remaining oil, and stir the mixture well.

Serve the salmon steaks surrounded by the pepper stew with the fresh tomato sauce on the side.

SUGGESTED ACCOMPANIMENT: *French bread.*

Red Mullet Marinated in Passion Fruit Juice

Serves 4
Working time: about 25 minutes
Total time: about 1 hour and 10 minutes

Calories **270**
Protein **39g**
Cholesterol **75mg**
Total fat **12g**
Saturated fat **1g**
Sodium **350mg**

4	*red mullet (about 250 g/8 oz each)*	*4*
8	*large fresh or vacuum-packed vine leaves*	*8*
	Marinade	
3	*passion fruit*	*3*
1 tbsp	*olive oil*	*1 tbsp*
2 tsp	*mixed dried herbs*	*2 tsp*
½ tsp	*salt*	*½ tsp*
	freshly ground black pepper	
	Garnish	
	black olives	
	lemon wedges	

As demonstrated on page 128, remove the fins and scales from the mullet, slit each fish along the belly and remove the viscera. Rinse the fish under cold water and pat them dry with paper towels.

To prepare the marinade, cut the passion fruit in half and scoop out the flesh into a small nylon sieve. Place the sieve over a bowl and extract the juice from the flesh with the back of a spoon. Add the oil, herbs, salt and pepper to the passion fruit juice and mix thoroughly. Transfer the marinade to a shallow dish. Place the mullet in the dish, then turn them in the marinade until well coated. Cover and marinate the fish for 1 hour.

Remove the mullet from the marinade and wrap each fish in two vine leaves. Place them in a shallow dish, then brush them with the remaining marinade. Cover the dish loosely with plastic film.

Microwave the mullet on high for 6 to 7 minutes, until cooked, carefully turning the fish half way through cooking.

Garnish with the black olives and lemon wedges. Serve immediately.

Prawn Teriyaki

Serves 4
Working time: about 20 minutes
Total time: about 30 minutes

Calories **125**
Protein **17g**
Cholesterol **130mg**
Total fat **1g**
Saturated fat **0g**
Sodium **405mg**

500 g	*large raw prawns, peeled and deveined*	*1 lb*
4 tbsp	*sweet sherry*	*4 tbsp*
2 tbsp	*low-sodium soy sauce or shoyu*	*2 tbsp*
1 tsp	*rice vinegar*	*1 tsp*
1	*garlic clove, finely chopped*	*1*
1	*slice wholemeal bread*	*1*
1 tsp	*cornflour*	*1 tsp*
12.5 cl	*fish stock (recipe, page 136) or dry white wine*	*4 fl oz*
1	*carrot, peeled and julienned*	*1*
3	*spring onions, trimmed and cut into 5 cm (2 inch) pieces, the pieces thinly sliced lengthwise*	*3*

Combine the sherry, soy sauce, vinegar and garlic in a bowl. Add the prawns and stir gently to coat them evenly. Marinate the prawns in the refrigerator for 20 minutes, stirring them from time to time.

Microwave the slice of bread on high for 2 minutes. Place the bread in a polythene bag and crush it into crumbs with a rolling pin.

Mix the cornflour with 1 tablespoon of the stock or wine. Strain the marinade into a glass bowl; stir in all but 2 tablespoons of the remaining stock or wine, along with the cornflour mixture. Microwave this sauce on high for 3 minutes. Stir the sauce until it is smooth, then set it aside.

Dip the prawns into the breadcrumbs to coat them on one side. Arrange the prawns, coated side up, in a shallow dish. Pour in the remaining stock or wine. Cover the dish and microwave it on high for 3 minutes. Rearrange the prawns, turning any uncooked pieces towards the edge of the dish.

Stir the carrot and spring onion strips into the sauce; pour the sauce around the prawns. Cover the dish again and cook it on medium high (70 per cent power) for 2 minutes. Allow the prawns to stand, covered, for another 2 minutes before transferring them to a serving dish. Spoon the sauce and vegetables around the prawns and serve immediately.

SUGGESTED ACCOMPANIMENT: *stir-fried rice.*

Mussels in Peppery Red-Wine Sauce

Serves 4 as a first course
Working (and total) time: about 15 minutes

Calories **165**
Protein **14g**
Cholesterol **75mg**
Total fat **6g**
Saturated fat **1g**
Sodium **315mg**

1 kg	*mussels, scrubbed and debearded*	*2 lb*
2	*large shallots, finely chopped*	*2*
2	*garlic cloves, finely chopped*	*2*
1	*bay leaf*	*1*
⅛ tsp	*dried thyme*	*⅛ tsp*
25	*black peppercorns (about ½ tsp), placed in a small polythene bag and crushed with the flat of a knife*	*25*
12.5 cl	*red wine*	*4 fl oz*
1 tbsp	*red wine vinegar*	*1 tbsp*
1 tbsp	*olive oil*	*1 tbsp*

Place half of the mussels, the shallots, garlic, bay leaf, thyme, peppercorns and wine in a deep dish. Cover the dish and microwave it on high for 2 minutes. Set aside the mussels that have opened. If there are any that remain tightly closed, re-cover the dish and microwave it on high for 30 seconds more. Again set aside the mussels that have opened. Microwave any remaining unopened mussels on high for 30 seconds; set the opened ones aside and discard any that stay closed. Add the remaining mussels to the dish and cook them in the same way.

When all of the mussels have been cooked, pour the vinegar and oil into the dish, cover it, and microwave the mixture on high for 2 minutes. Return the mussels to the dish, stirring to coat them with the liquid, and cover the dish once more. Microwave on high for 1 minute to heat the mussels through. Serve the mussels in their shells directly from the dish, or transfer them to a serving bowl along with their sauce.

Crab Meat with Tomatoes, Mushrooms and Garlic

Serves 4
Working (and total) time: about 25 minutes

Calories **215**
Protein **22g**
Cholesterol **85mg**
Total fat **5g**
Saturated fat **1g**
Sodium **245mg**

500 g	*crab meat, picked over*	*1 lb*
250 g	*mushrooms, wiped clean and sliced*	*8 oz*
6	*shallots, finely chopped*	*6*
6	*garlic cloves, finely chopped*	*6*
6 tbsp	*dry sherry*	*6 tbsp*
6 tbsp	*dry white wine*	*6 tbsp*
⅛ tsp	*crushed red pepper flakes*	*⅛ tsp*
500 g	*ripe tomatoes, skinned, seeded and chopped*	*1 lb*
2 tbsp	*chopped fresh parsley*	*2 tbsp*
1 tbsp	*virgin olive oil*	*1 tbsp*

Combine the mushrooms, shallots, garlic, sherry, wine and crushed red pepper flakes in a baking dish. Cover and microwave on high for 8 minutes, stirring once mid-way through the cooking time. Add the crab meat, tomatoes, parsley and oil, and toss well. Cover the dish tightly, microwave on high for 2 minutes and serve immediately. (If you prefer, spoon individual portions into ceramic or natural crab shells before serving.)

SUGGESTED ACCOMPANIMENT: *batavian endive salad.*

Oysters and Pasta Shells in Mornay Sauce

Serves 4
Working (and total) time: about 20 minutes

Calories **335**
Protein **21g**
Cholesterol **90mg**
Total fat **12g**
Saturated fat **4g**
Sodium **315mg**

250 g	*shucked oysters, drained*	*8 oz*
125 g	*medium pasta shells*	*4 oz*
1 tbsp	*safflower oil*	*1 tbsp*
1 tbsp	*finely chopped shallot*	*1 tbsp*
60 g	*Gruyère cheese, coarsely grated*	*2 oz*
2 tbsp	*flour*	*2 tbsp*
¼ litre	*semi-skimmed milk*	*8 fl oz*
	grated nutmeg	
⅛ tsp	*salt*	*⅛ tsp*
	white pepper	
1 tbsp	*fresh breadcrumbs*	*1 tbsp*
½ tsp	*paprika*	*½ tsp*

Cook the pasta in 1 litre (1¾ pints) of boiling water with ¼ teaspoon of salt; start testing the shells after 10 minutes and cook them until they are *al dente*. Drain, put them in a bowl and cover them with cold water.

Place the oil and shallot in another bowl, cover with plastic film or a lid, and microwave it on high for 45 seconds. Toss the cheese with the flour, evenly coating the cheese, and add this mixture to the bowl. Stir in the milk, a pinch of nutmeg, the salt and some white pepper. Cover the bowl again, leaving a slight gap to allow steam to escape, and microwave it on high for 3 minutes. Remove from the oven and stir the sauce.

Drain the reserved pasta and combine it with the sauce. Gently stir in the oysters, then transfer the mixture to a shallow baking dish. Cover the dish and microwave it on medium (50 per cent power) for 5 minutes. Remove the dish from the oven and stir to blend the oyster liquid into the sauce. Combine the breadcrumbs with the paprika and sprinkle them over the top. Serve immediately.

SUGGESTED ACCOMPANIMENT: *sautéed sweet red peppers.*

Lemon Sole Paupiettes with Ginger and Dill

Serves 4 as a starter
Working (and total) time: about 45 minutes

Calories **230**
Protein **32g**
Cholesterol **95mg**
Total fat **9g**
Saturated fat **4g**
Sodium **370mg**

2	*large lemon soles (about 500 to 750 g/ 1 to 1½ lb each)*	2
30 g	*unsalted butter, softened*	1 oz
15 g	*fresh ginger root, peeled and very finely chopped*	½ oz
1½ tbsp	*chopped fresh dill*	1½ tbsp
¼ tsp	*salt*	¼ tsp
	freshly ground black pepper	
1 tsp	*lemon juice*	1 tsp
500 g	*courgettes, cut into julienne strips*	1 lb
1 tsp	*cornflour*	1 tsp
	lemon twists for garnish	

Skin and fillet the soles as demonstrated on pages 129 and 131. Trim the "frilly" edge from each fillet to neaten, then roughly chop the trimmings and set aside. Blend the butter with the chopped ginger, 1 tablespoon of the dill, the salt, pepper and lemon juice. Mix in the reserved sole trimmings.

Lay the sole fillets on the work surface skinned-side uppermost, then spread each one with ginger and dill butter. Roll up each fillet, from head to tail, to enclose the butter and form a neat paupiette. Place the paupiettes in a shallow dish. Loosely cover the dish with plastic film, and set aside.

Place the courgettes in another shallow dish, then season with salt and pepper. Cover the dish with plastic film, pulling back one corner to vent. Microwave the courgettes on high for 5 to 6 minutes, until they are barely cooked. Remove them from the microwave, cover and keep warm while the sole is cooking.

With the microwave on high, cook the paupiettes for 4 to 5 minutes, turning them half way through cooking. Carefully arrange the paupiettes and courgettes on a hot serving dish. Cover and keep warm.

Blend the cornflour with a little cold water. Stir the cornflour into the fish juices, then microwave on high for 1½ minutes until the sauce thickens, stirring with a wire whisk every 30 seconds. Glaze the paupiettes with the sauce, sprinkle with the remaining chopped dill, and garnish with lemon twists. Serve immediately.

Roulades of Plaice with Seaweed, Spinach and Rice

Serves 4
Working time: about 20 minutes
Total time: about 45 minutes

Calories **245**
Protein **25g**
Cholesterol **55mg**
Total fat **2g**
Saturated fat **1g**
Sodium **665mg**

500 g	*plaice or sole fillets, cut lengthwise into 8 equal pieces*	*1 lb*
90 g	*rice*	*3 oz*
30 cl	*unsalted tomato juice*	*½ pint*
½ tsp	*fennel seeds*	*½ tsp*
¼ tsp	*salt*	*¼ tsp*
250 g	*fresh spinach*	*8 oz*
	white pepper	
2	*sheets nori (dried roasted seaweed)*	*2*
1 tbsp	*cornflour*	*1 tbsp*
¼ litre	*fish stock (recipe, page 136)*	*8 fl oz*
2 tbsp	*mirin (sweetened Japanese rice wine) or cream sherry*	*2 tbsp*
2 tbsp	*low-sodium soy sauce or shoyu*	*2 tbsp*
2 tsp	*rice vinegar*	*2 tsp*
4 or 5	*drops Tabasco sauce*	*4 or 5*
2 tbsp	*chopped parsley*	*2 tbsp*

To prepare the filling, combine the rice, tomato juice, fennel seeds and salt in a 1 litre (2 pint) measuring jug or glass bowl and cover it. Microwave the filling on high for 12 minutes, then set it aside, still covered.

Wash and stem the spinach. Put the spinach with just the water that clings to it into a 2 litre (3½ pint) baking dish. Cover the dish with plastic film and microwave it on high for 3 minutes. Remove the spinach from the oven and let it cool.

Rinse the fillets under cold running water and pat them dry with paper towels. Lay the fillets side by side, with their darker sides up, on a work surface; season them with the white pepper. Spread a thin layer of the rice filling on each fillet. Cut a strip of *nori* to fit each fillet. Lay the strips in place on the rice, then cover each strip of *nori* with some spinach. Roll each fillet into a roulade, rolling end to end as you would do to form a swiss roll.

Mix the cornflour with 2 tablespoons of the stock; then, in the same dish you used to cook the spinach, stir together the remaining stock, the cornflour mixture, the mirin, soy sauce, vinegar and Tabasco sauce. Microwave the mixture on high for 3 minutes; stir the resulting sauce until it is smooth. Lay the roulades in the sauce, their seam sides down; they should be close but not touching. Cover the dish and microwave it on high for 6 minutes. Let the dish stand for 3 minutes. Just before serving the roulades, spoon some of the sauce over them and garnish them with the parsley.

SUGGESTED ACCOMPANIMENT: *red cabbage salad.*

Haddock with Endive and Bacon

Serves 4
Working (and total) time: about 20 minutes

Calories **150**
Protein **24g**
Cholesterol **70mg**
Total fat **3g**
Saturated fat **1g**
Sodium **270mg**

500 g	*haddock fillets (or cod or coley)*	*1 lb*
2	*garlic cloves, finely chopped*	*2*
2 tbsp	*fresh lemon juice*	*2 tbsp*
1 tsp	*fresh rosemary, or ¼ tsp dried rosemary, crumbled*	*1 tsp*
	freshly ground black pepper	
2	*rashers streaky bacon, rind removed*	*2*
1	*endive (about 500 g/1 lb), trimmed, washed and cut into 2.5 cm (1 inch) pieces*	*1*
⅛ tsp	*salt*	*⅛ tsp*

Rinse the haddock under cold running water and pat it dry with paper towels. Cut it into four serving pieces. Rub the fish with half of the garlic, 1 tablespoon of the lemon juice, the rosemary and a generous grinding of pepper. Set the fish aside.

Cut the rashers in half crosswise and put them in the bottom of a large dish. Microwave the bacon on high until done but not crisp — about 2 minutes. Lay a strip of bacon on top of each piece of fish.

Add the remaining garlic to the bacon fat in the dish. Add the endive to the dish with the remaining lemon juice, the salt and some pepper. Toss the endive to distribute the seasonings, then mound it in the centre of the dish. Microwave the dish on high for 2 minutes. Briefly toss the endive again and then microwave it on high until it wilts — about 2 minutes more.

Lay the fish on top of the endive. Microwave the fish on medium (50 per cent power) until the flesh is opaque — 5 to 6 minutes. Remove the dish from the oven and spoon the juices that have collected in the bottom into a small saucepan. Boil the juices rapidly until only 2 tablespoons of liquid remain; pour the sauce over the fish and serve at once.

SUGGESTED ACCOMPANIMENT: *curried rice.*

Swordfish Steaks with Lemon, Orange and Lime

Serves 4
Working time: about 15 minutes
Total time: about 35 minutes

Calories **250**
Protein **30g**
Cholesterol **75mg**
Total fat **12g**
Saturated fat **3g**
Sodium **155mg**

750 g	*swordfish steak (or shark or tuna), trimmed and cut into quarters*	*1½ lb*
1	*lemon*	*1*
1	*orange*	*1*
1	*lime*	*1*
1½ tbsp	*virgin olive oil*	*1½ tbsp*
1 tsp	*fresh rosemary, crushed, or ½ tsp dried rosemary*	*1 tsp*
1	*bay leaf, crushed*	*1*
½ tsp	*fresh thyme, or ¼ tsp dried thyme*	*½ tsp*
¼ tsp	*fennel seeds*	*¼ tsp*
⅛ tsp	*cayenne pepper*	*⅛ tsp*

Rinse the swordfish steaks under cold running water and pat them dry with paper towels. Cut the lemon, orange and lime in half. Cut one half of each fruit into wedges and reserve the wedges for garnish. Squeeze the juice from the other halves into a small bowl. Pour the citrus juices over the fish and let the fish marinate at room temperature for 30 minutes.

While the fish is marinating, pour the oil into a 12.5 cl (4 fl oz) ramekin. Add the rosemary, bay leaf, thyme, fennel seeds and cayenne pepper. Cover the ramekin with plastic film and microwave it on high for 2 minutes. Set the seasoned oil aside until the fish finishes marinating.

Preheat the microwave browning dish on high for the maximum time allowed in the manufacturer's instruction manual. While the dish is heating, brush the seasoned oil on both sides of each swordfish steak. When the dish is ready, set the steaks on it and cook them on high for 90 seconds. Turn the steaks over and cook them for 90 seconds more — they will still be translucent in the centre. Let the steaks stand for 1 minute, then serve them with the fruit wedges.

SUGGESTED ACCOMPANIMENTS: *burghul; red lettuce salad.*

EDITOR'S NOTE: *If you do not have a microwave browning dish, microwave the steaks in an uncovered baking dish for 5 to 6 minutes.*

East African Fish Stew

Serves 4
Working time: about 20 minutes
Total time: about 35 minutes

Calories **435**
Protein **22g**
Cholesterol **20mg**
Total fat **8g**
Saturated fat **1g**
Sodium **185mg**

250 g	*fresh tuna (or swordfish)*	*8 oz*
1 tbsp	*safflower oil*	*1 tbsp*
1	*large onion, chopped*	*1*
2	*garlic cloves, finely chopped*	*2*
1 tsp	*ground turmeric*	*1 tsp*
400 g	*canned whole tomatoes, coarsely chopped, juice reserved*	*14 oz*
1 tsp	*red wine vinegar*	*1 tsp*
1 tsp	*brown sugar*	*1 tsp*
20	*saffron threads*	*20*
⅛ tsp	*crushed red pepper flakes*	*⅛ tsp*
140 g	*long-grain rice*	*4½ oz*
¼ tsp	*salt*	*¼ tsp*
2	*waxy potatoes (about 350 g/12 oz), peeled and cut into 5 mm (¼ inch) cubes*	*2*
75 g	*shelled peas*	*2½ oz*
2 tbsp	*fresh lemon juice*	*2 tbsp*
2 tbsp	*garam masala*	*2 tbsp*

In a large glass bowl, stir together the oil, onion, garlic and turmeric. Cover the bowl and microwave it on high until the onions are limp — 2 to 3 minutes. Stir in the tomatoes and their juice, the vinegar, brown sugar, saffron threads and red pepper flakes. Cover the bowl and microwave it on high for 10 minutes.

Bring ½ litre (16 fl oz) of water to the boil in a small saucepan, then add the rice and salt. Cover the pan and cook the rice over medium heat until all the water has been absorbed — about 20 minutes.

While the rice is cooking, finish the stew. Rinse the fish under cold running water, pat it dry with paper towels and cut it into 1 cm (½ inch) cubes. Add the potatoes to the onion-tomato mixture. Cover the bowl and microwave it on high for 5 minutes. Next add the tuna; cover the bowl and microwave it on high for 10 minutes more, stirring the contents half way through the cooking time. Finally, add the peas and lemon juice and cook the stew on high, covered, for 1 minute.

To serve, divide the rice evenly between four bowls. Ladle one quarter of the stew over each serving of rice. Serve the garam masala separately.

EDITOR'S NOTE: *Garam masala, an Indian spice mixture, can be made at home by combining 1 teaspoon each of ground cumin, turmeric, cardamom and coriander with ½ teaspoon each of ground cloves, mace and cayenne pepper and ¼ teaspoon of cinnamon.*

Techniques

Dressing a Round Fish

1 *CUTTING OFF THE FINS. Rinse the fish under cold running water, but do not dry it. With a pair of kitchen scissors, cut off the fins and discard them. If you intend to cook the fish whole, trim the tail short enough to allow the fish to fit in the cooking vessel.*

2 *REMOVING THE SCALES. Cover the fish with polythene. Hold firmly on to the tail with one hand to keep the fish flat on the work surface. Working from the tail to the head under the polythene, use a fish scaler to scrape off the scales. If you do not have a scaler, a sturdy tablespoon will do.*

3 *CUTTING OUT THE GILLS. If you plan to cook the fish with the head on, you must remove the gills to avoid a bitter taste. Lift the gill covering on one side, snip around the dark red gill with kitchen scissors to remove it. Discard the gill and repeat the procedure for the other gill.*

4 *SLITTING THE BELLY. Pierce the underside at the anal vent with the tip of a knife and slit the belly towards the head, keeping the cut shallow enough to avoid cutting into the viscera. Alternatively, cut open with kitchen scissors. (If the head is to be removed, slit the belly from front to vent.)*

5 GUTTING. Reach into the belly with your fingers and pull out the viscera. Use a knife or scissors to sever and remove any visceral attachments; then break the membrane lining the belly on either side of the backbone to release any accumulated blood. Thoroughly rinse out the belly cavity and gill area.

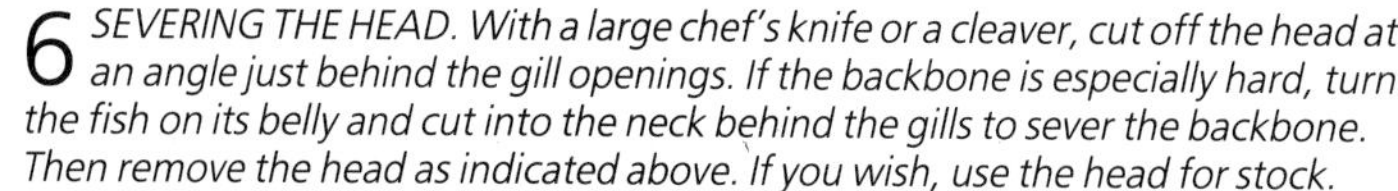

6 SEVERING THE HEAD. With a large chef's knife or a cleaver, cut off the head at an angle just behind the gill openings. If the backbone is especially hard, turn the fish on its belly and cut into the neck behind the gills to sever the backbone. Then remove the head as indicated above. If you wish, use the head for stock.

A Rapid Way to Skin a Sole

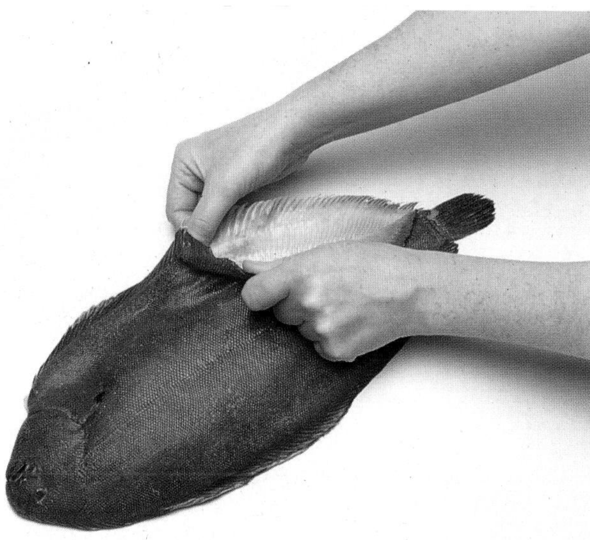

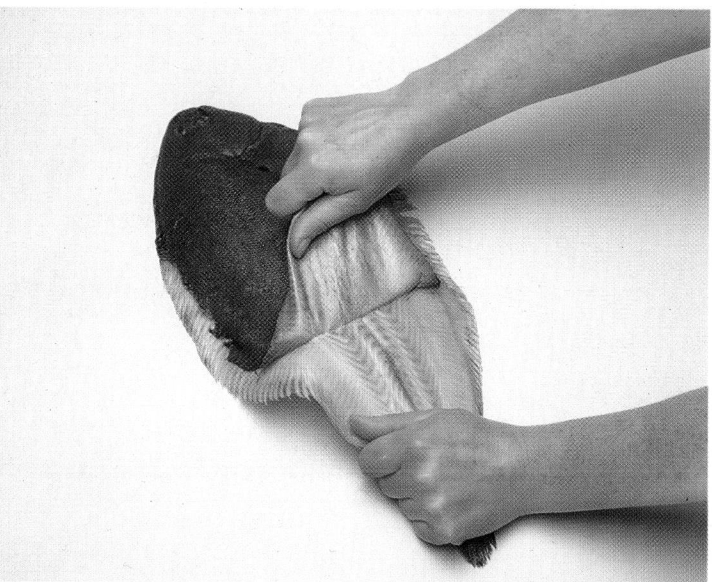

1 STARTING THE OPERATION. Lay the fish dark side uppermost on a cutting board. With a sharp knife, cut across the skin where the tail joins the body. Starting at the cut, use your thumbnail to prise away the skin along the edge as far as the head (above). Repeat along the other edge.

2 PEELING OFF THE SKIN. Grasp the flap of the skin in one hand; with the other hold down the tail. Firmly and decisively, pull the skin towards the head until it comes away. If removing the white skin, turn the fish over and repeat the process.

Filleting a Round Fish

1 *CUTTING BEHIND THE HEAD. Snip off the fins, and scale and gut the fish. Rinse it thoroughly under cold running water, making sure the abdominal cavity is clean. Place a filleting or flexible boning knife at a diagonal behind the head of the fish and cut down to the backbone without severing it.*

2 *CUTTING ALONG THE BACKBONE. Position the fish on the work surface with the tail pointing towards you. Hold the fish steady on the work surface and place the knife just above the bony ridge of the spine. Cut along the length of the backbone, from the neck to the tail, about 1 cm (½ inch) deep.*

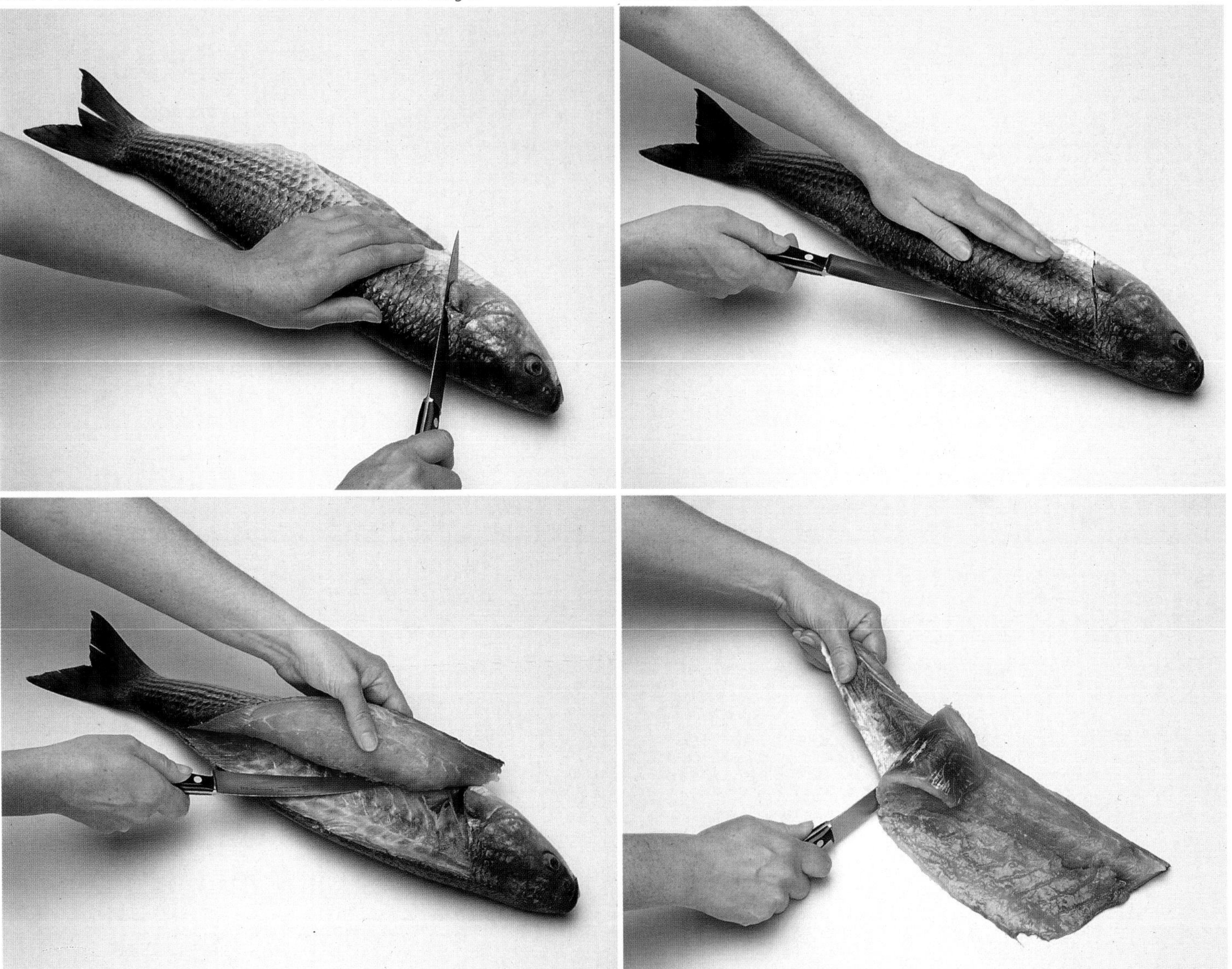

3 *REMOVING THE FILLETS. Insert the knife into the cut and trim the flesh from the rib cage with short strokes, cutting parallel to the bones. Peel back the flesh with your other hand as you go, until the fillet comes away in a strip. Flip the fish over, turn the head towards you, and repeat the procedure.*

4 *SKINNING THE FILLETS. Place a fillet skin side down on the work surface. Trim a small piece of flesh from the tail end. Holding on to the exposed skin, place a knife (here, a slicer) between the flesh and the skin. With the blade angled slightly downwards, run the knife along the skin to separate the fillet.*

Filleting a Flat Fish

1 *CUTTING BEHIND THE HEAD. Rinse the fish under cold running water, but do not dry it. With a filleting or flexible boning knife, make a V-shaped cut behind the head, slicing down the backbone without severing it. Around the belly, cut through the flesh, taking care not to pierce the viscera.*

2 *CUTTING DOWN THE BACKBONE. Position the fish on the work surface with the tail pointing towards you. Place the knife at the point of the "V" and make a straight cut down the centre line of the fish from the neck to the tail, following the ridge of the backbone.*

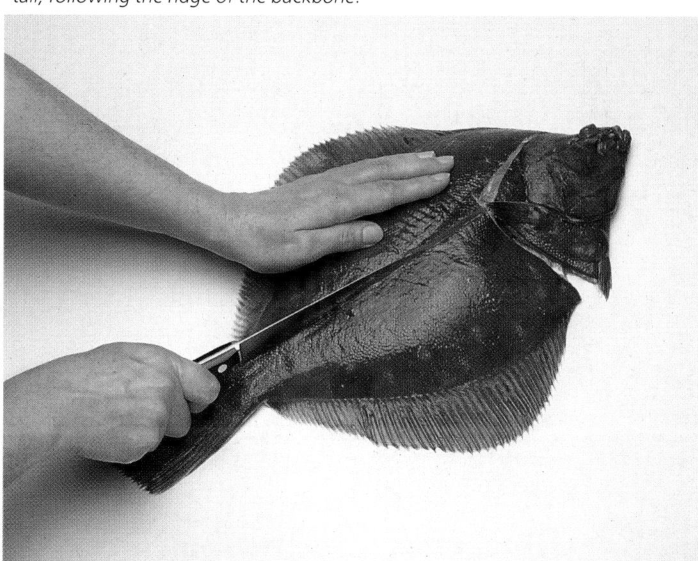

3 *REMOVING THE FILLETS. Insert the knife into the cut and trim a fillet from the rib cage with short strokes, cutting parallel to the bones. Peel back the flesh as you go, until the fillet comes away in a strip. Rotate the fish to fillet the other side. Then flip the fish over and repeat the procedures.*

4 *SKINNING THE FILLETS. Place a fillet skin side down on the work surface. Trim a small piece of flesh from the tail end. Holding on to the exposed skin with your fingers, place a knife between the flesh and the skin. With the blade angled downwards, run the knife along the skin to separate the fillet.*

Preparing a Squid for Cooking

1 *SEPARATING THE POUCH AND TENTACLES. Working over a bowl of water or a sink, hold the squid's pouch in one hand and its tentacles in the other. Gently pull the tentacles until the viscera separate from the inside of the pouch. Set the tentacles aside, with the head and viscera still attached.*

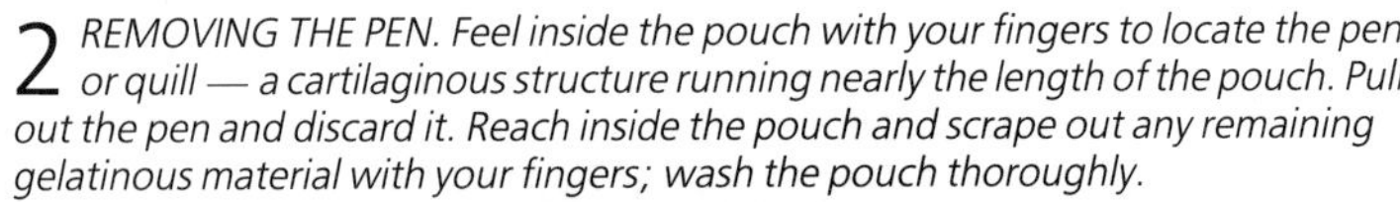

2 *REMOVING THE PEN. Feel inside the pouch with your fingers to locate the pen, or quill — a cartilaginous structure running nearly the length of the pouch. Pull out the pen and discard it. Reach inside the pouch and scrape out any remaining gelatinous material with your fingers; wash the pouch thoroughly.*

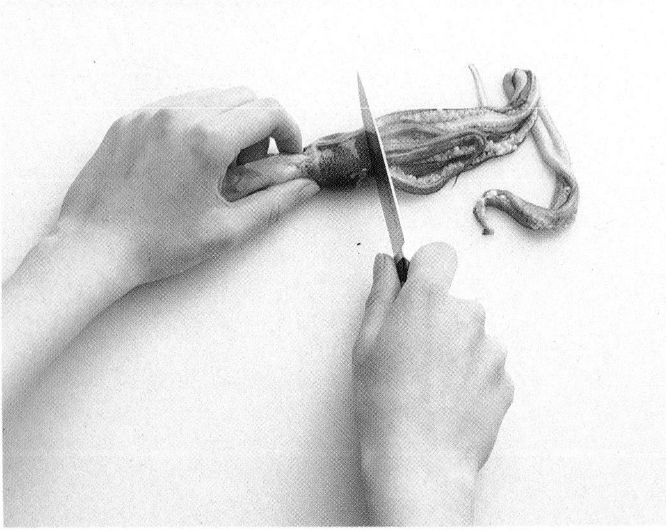

3 *SKINNING THE POUCH. Starting at the open end of the pouch, use your fingers to pull the mottled purplish skin away from the pale flesh. Continue peeling off the skin from the pouch; discard the skin. Rinse the pouch again, then set it aside in a bowl of fresh cold water.*

4 *CUTTING OFF THE TENTACLES. Lay the viscera, head and tentacles on a cutting board. Sever the tentacles from the head below the eyes; the tentacles should remain joined together by a narrow band of flesh. Discard the head and viscera. If any of the bony beak remains in the tentacle section, squeeze it out.*

Preparing a Crab

1 *REMOVING THE CLAWS AND LEGS. Place a cooked crab underside up on a work surface. With your fingers, break the claws from the body by twisting them against the direction in which the pincers face. In the same way, detach the eight legs, snapping them off as close as possible to the shell.*

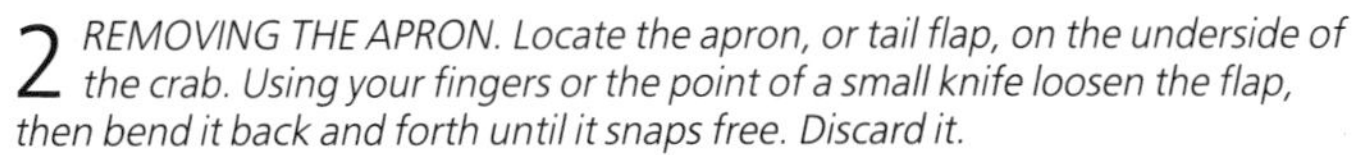

2 *REMOVING THE APRON. Locate the apron, or tail flap, on the underside of the crab. Using your fingers or the point of a small knife loosen the flap, then bend it back and forth until it snaps free. Discard it.*

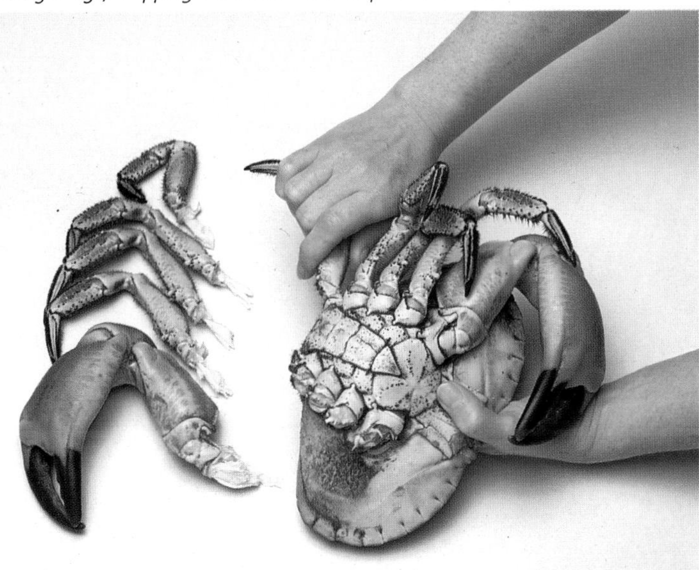

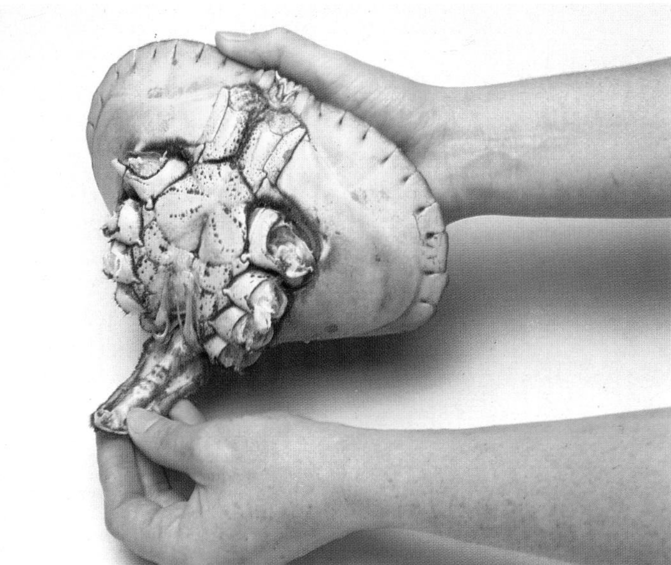

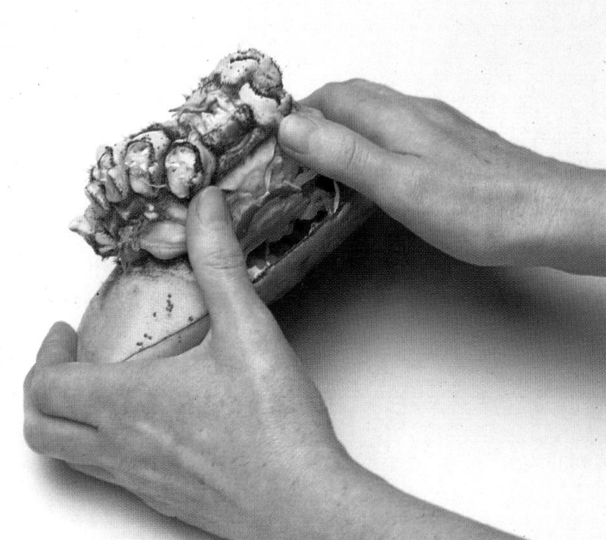

3 *OPENING THE CRAB. Holding the crab on its side with the tail end uppermost, grip the shell with both hands and push the underside free with your thumbs. Pull the two sections apart and set the shell aside.*

4 *REMOVING THE GILLS. From the edges of the underside pull away the soft elongated gills and the feathery wisps and discard them. Check that none of the gills have fallen into the shell.* ►

5 *SCOOPING OUT THE SHELL. Remove the small bag-like stomach sac and its appendages which are located just behind the crab's mouth. Discard them. Scoop out the meat from the shell and reserve it.*

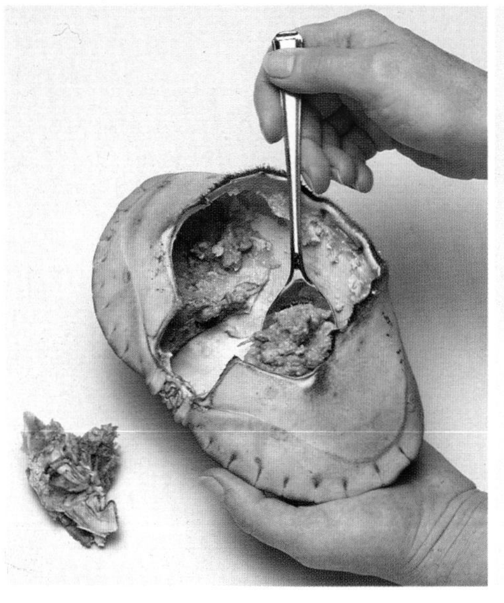

6 *EXTRACTING THE BODY MEAT. With a heavy kitchen knife split the underside in two. With the tip of a small knife, pick out the white flaky meat from all the many crevices.*

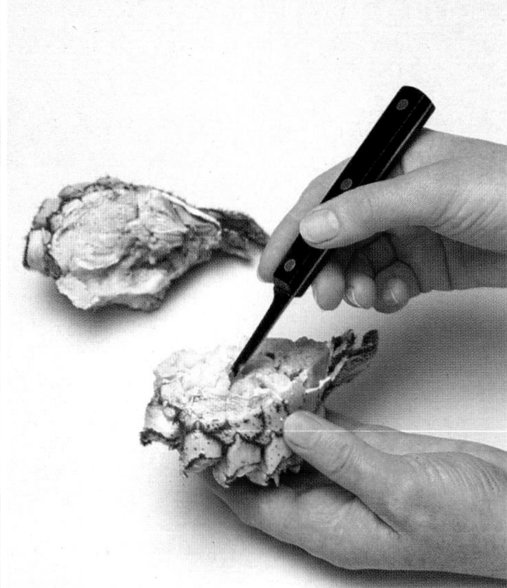

7 *CRACKING THE CLAWS. Crack the shell of each claw with a mallet. Peel away the shell and extract the flesh and the meat concealed in the pincers. Repeat this procedure for each of the legs.*

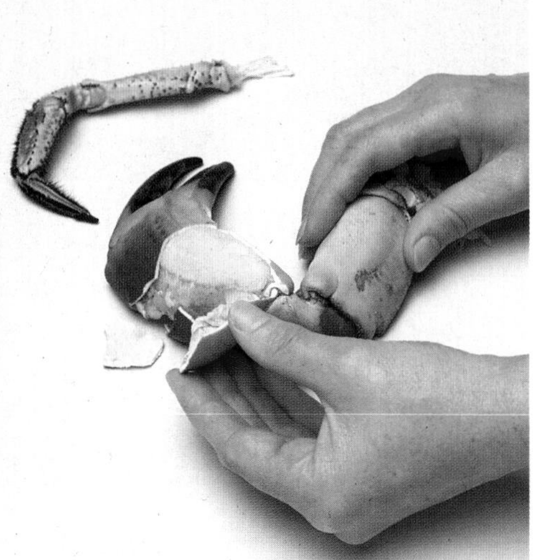

Preparing a Lobster

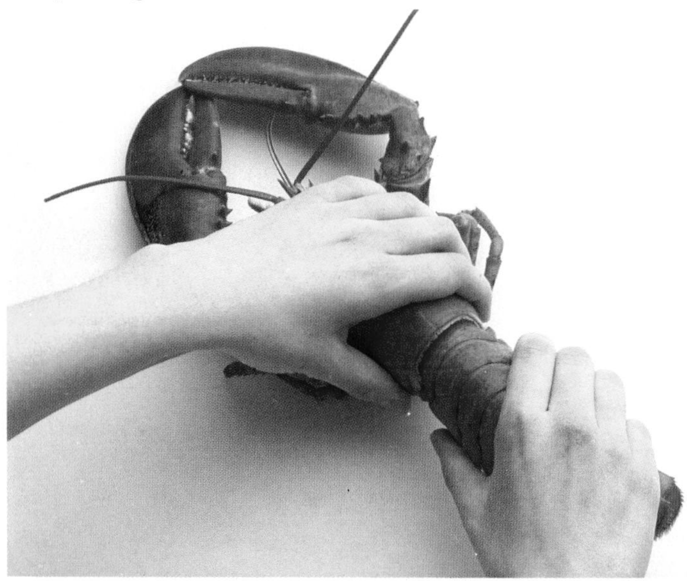

1 *SEPARATING THE TAIL FROM THE BODY. Place a cooked lobster right side up on a work surface. Hold the thorax, or body, portion firmly with one hand, and with the other hand twist the tail section, pulling it free of the body.*

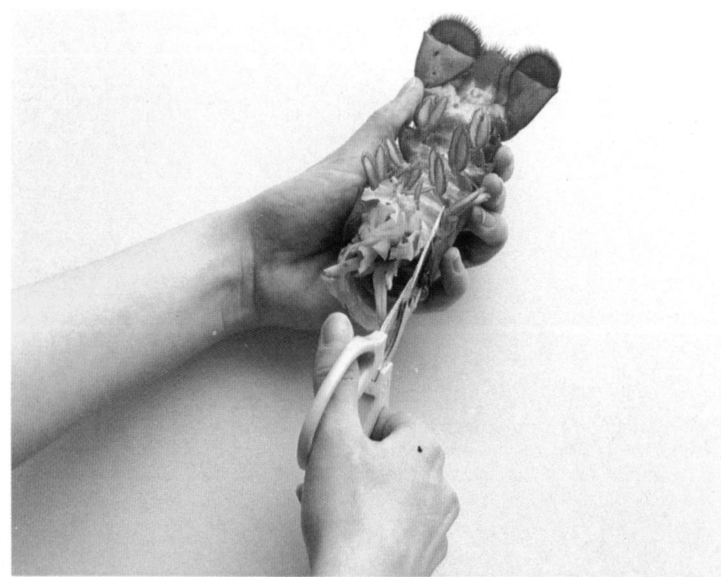

2 *EXTRACTING THE TAIL MEAT. Holding the tail section upside down in the palm of one hand, snip down both sides of the thin shell with kitchen scissors. Be careful not to cut into the meat beneath. Lift the meat from the tail in one piece and set it aside.*

3 REMOVING THE CLAWS AND LEGS. *With your fingers, grasp a claw near its base and twist it off. Twist off the other claw and the eight small legs. Break each leg apart at the central joint; then, with a small pick or a skewer, remove the slivers of flesh inside.*

4 SEPARATING THE CLAW AT THE JOINT. *Holding the claw by the pincer in one hand, firmly grasp the first joint with the other hand and twist it to free it from the pincer. Repeat the procedure to separate the other claw at its joint.*

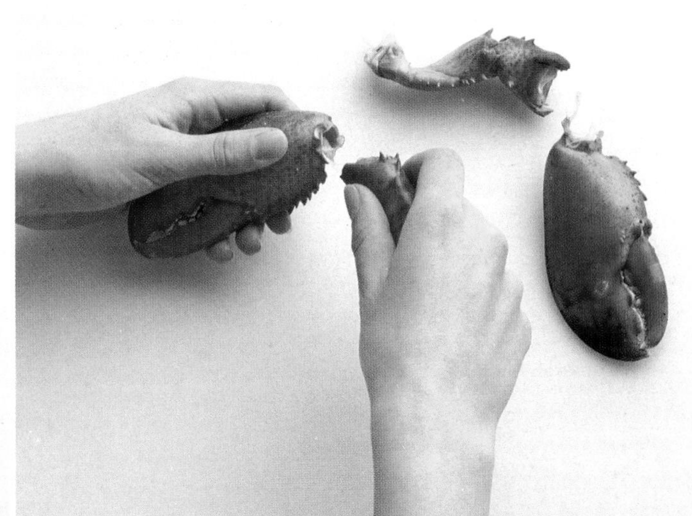

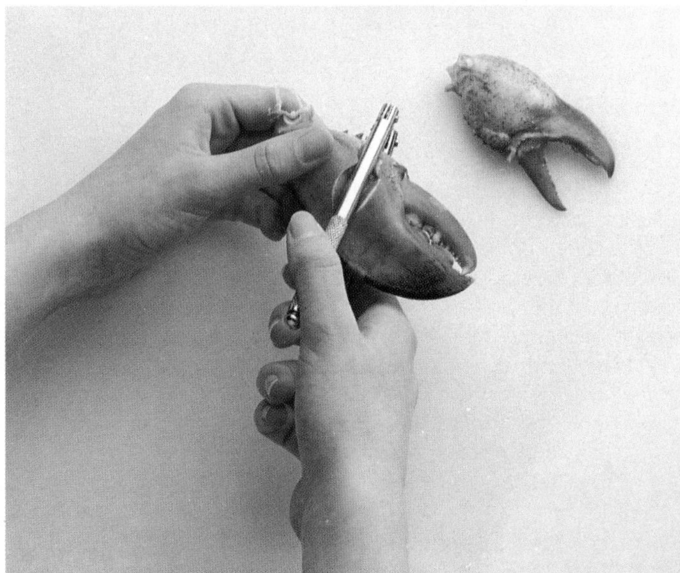

5 CRACKING THE CLAWS. *With a nutcracker or a pair of pliers held at a slight diagonal to the claw's widest point, crack a claw. Lift away any shell fragments and carefully pull out the claw meat. Crack the joint segments and remove the meat. Repeat the procedure with the other claw.*

6 SPLITTING THE BODY. *Place the body on its back and split it down the centre with a large knife. Discard the viscera and the sand sac found near the head. Scrape out the edible greenish tomalley, or liver, and the reddish orange coral, if it is present. Use a pick or fork to extract any meaty bits from the body.*

Court-Bouillon

Makes about 3 litres (5 pints)
Working time: about 10 minutes
Total time: about 35 minutes

4	*onions, thinly sliced*	4
3	*sticks celery, thinly sliced*	3
2	*carrots, peeled and thinly sliced*	2
10	*parsley stems*	10
3	*fresh thyme sprigs, or 1 tsp dried thyme*	3
4	*garlic cloves, crushed*	4
2	*bay leaves*	2
1 tsp	*aniseeds or fennel seeds (optional)*	1 tsp
35 cl	*dry white wine*	12 fl oz
4 tbsp	*white wine vinegar*	4 tbsp
5	*peppercorns, cracked*	5

Put the onions, celery, carrots, parsley, thyme, garlic, bay leaves and aniseeds or fennel seeds, if you are using them, into a large, non-reactive stockpot. Pour in 3 litres (5 pints) of water, cover the pot, and bring the liquid to the boil. Reduce the heat and simmer the liquid, with the lid slightly ajar, for 15 minutes.

Add the wine, vinegar and peppercorns, and simmer the court-bouillon for 15 minutes more. Strain the liquid through a fine sieve into a bowl or a clean pan before using it.

Fish Stock

Makes about 2 litres (3½ pints)
Working time: about 15 minutes
Total time: about 40 minutes

1 kg	*lean fish bones, fins and tails discarded, the bones rinsed thoroughly and chopped into large pieces*	2 lb
2	*onions, thinly sliced*	2
2	*sticks celery, chopped*	2
1	*carrot, peeled and thinly sliced*	1
½ litre	*dry white wine*	16 fl oz
2 tbsp	*fresh lemon juice*	2 tbsp
1	*leek (optional), trimmed, split, washed thoroughly to remove all grit, and sliced*	1
3	*garlic cloves (optional), crushed*	3
10	*parsley stems*	10
3	*fresh thyme sprigs, or 1 tsp dried thyme*	3
1	*bay leaf*	1
5	*black peppercorns, cracked*	5

Put the fish bones, onions, celery, carrot, wine, lemon juice, 2 litres (3½ pints) of water, and the leek and garlic, if you are using them, in a large non-reactive stockpot. Bring the liquid to the boil, then reduce the heat to medium to maintain a strong simmer. Skim off all the scum that rises to the surface.

Add the parsley, thyme, bay leaf and peppercorns. Reduce the heat to medium low and simmer the stock for 20 minutes.

Strain the stock through a fine sieve lined with muslin. Allow the stock to cool before refrigerating or freezing it.

EDITOR'S NOTE: *The stock will keep for 3 days in the refrigerator. Stored in small, well-sealed freezer containers, the stock may be kept frozen for as long as two months.*

Because the bones from oilier fish produce a strong flavour, be sure to use only the bones from lean fish. Sole, plaice, turbot and other flat fish are best.

Glossary

Aniseed: the liquorice-flavoured seed of a plant native to the Middle East. It is used in certain curries and to flavour sauces.
Anisette: a clear, sweet liqueur made from herbs and seeds, among them aniseeds.
Apron: the triangular or T-shaped flap found on the underside of a crab's shell. The apron varies in size or shape depending on the species.
Balsamic vinegar: a mild, dark red, intensely fragrant wine-based vinegar made in northern Italy. Traditionally, the vinegar is aged for several years in a series of casks made of various woods.
Bamboo shoots: the cream-coloured, crisp young shoots of the bamboo plant. Raw bamboo shoots are poisonous; they must be cooked before eating.
Basil: a leafy herb in the mint family, with a strong, pungent aroma when fresh, often used in Italian cooking. If they are covered with olive oil and refrigerated in a tightly sealed container, whole fresh basil leaves may be kept for several months.
Bass: see Sea bass.
Bay leaves: the aromatic leaves of *Laurus nobilis*, a Mediterranean evergreen, used fresh or dried for flavouring stews and stocks. Dried bay leaves when broken have very sharp edges and can injure internally, so should be removed before serving.
Black vinegar, Chinese: (also called Chenkong vinegar, Chinkiang vinegar): a dark vinegar made from fermented rice. Balsamic vinegar may be used as a substitute.
Blanch: to partially cook food by briefly immersing it in boiling water. Blanching makes such thin-skinned vegetables as tomatoes easier to peel; it can also mellow strong flavours.
Bream: see Freshwater bream; Sea bream.
Brill: a flat fish that looks like a smaller version of turbot. The flesh of brill is not as fine as that of turbot, but it is still good to eat.
Calorie (or kilocalorie): precise measure of the energy food supplies when broken down for use in the body.
Caramelize: to heat sugar until it turns brown and syrupy. Also, the process whereby naturally occurring sugars in such foods as shallots and onions change to caramel, contributing a rich flavour.
Cardamom: the bittersweet, aromatic dried seeds or whole pods of a plant in the ginger family. Cardamom seeds may be used whole or ground.
Carp: a freshwater fish, ranging from 1.5 to 9 kg (3 to 20 lb), with coarse, rich flesh. The darker flesh is generally cut away and discarded.
Cayenne pepper: a fiery powder ground from the seeds and pods of various red chili peppers. It is used in small amounts to heighten other flavours.
Chervil: a lacy, slightly anise-flavoured herb often used as a companion to other herbs, such as tarragon and chives. Because long cooking may kill its flavour, chervil should be added at the last minute.
Chicory: a small, cylindrical vegetable, composed of many tightly wrapped white to pale-yellow leaves. It can be cooked, or eaten raw in salads.
Chili paste: a paste of chilies, salt and other ingredients, among them garlic and black beans. Several kinds are available in Asian shops.
Chili peppers: a variety of hot red or green peppers. Serranos and jalapeños are small fresh green chilies that are extremely hot. Anchos are dried poblano chilies that are mildly hot and dark red in colour. Fresh or dried, chili peppers contain volatile oils that can irritate the skin and eyes; they must be handled with extreme care (caution, page 45).
Chinese black vinegar: see Black vinegar, Chinese.
Chinese cabbage (also called Chinese leaves): an elongated cabbage resembling cos lettuce, with long, broad ribs and crinkled, light green to white leaves.
Cholesterol: a wax-like substance that is manufactured in the human body and also found in foods of animal origin. Although a certain amount of cholesterol is necessary for proper body functioning, an excess can accumulate in the arteries, contributing to heart disease. See also Monounsaturated fats; Polyunsaturated fats; Saturated fats.
Chutney: a pickle of Indian origin that can be made of fruits, vegetables, spices, vinegar and sugar. It is served cooked or raw, traditionally with curry. The cooked variety is available bottled.
Clam: a bivalve mollusc with greyish to whitish shells, found primarily along the Atlantic and Pacific coasts. Small hard-shell clams are also known as quahogs. See also Littleneck clam; Purge.
Cod: a salt-water fish, normally weighing between 3 and 7.5 kg (6 and 15 lb), that is caught year round in the Atlantic and Pacific. Its lean, white flesh flakes easily when cooked. See also Coley; Haddock; Hake.
Coley (also called saithe): a smaller relative of cod, with a darker, pinkish-grey tint to the flesh, found in the northern Atlantic Ocean. The flesh is lean and can be coarse.
Coral: the edible roe of the scallop, lobster or crab.
Coriander (also called cilantro): the pungent, peppery leaves of the coriander plant or its earthy tasting dried seeds. It is a common seasoning in Middle-Eastern, Oriental and Latin-American cookery.
Court-bouillon: a flavoured liquid used for poaching fish or shellfish. It may contain aromatic vegetables, herbs, wine or milk.
Couscous: cereal processed from semolina into pellets, traditionally steamed and served in the classic North African stew of the same name.
Crab: a crustacean with five pairs of jointed legs, the first of which have pincers. It is often sold cooked because of its high perishability.
Crawfish: see Spiny lobster.
Crayfish: a freshwater crustacean similar in appearance to lobster, except that it is much smaller — its body measures only from 8.5 to 12.5 cm (3½ to 5 inches). Crayfish are called *écrevisse* in France and elsewhere.
Cumin: the aromatic seeds of an umbelliferous plant similar to fennel used, whole or powdered, as a spice, especially in Indian and Latin-American dishes. Toasting gives it a nutty flavour.
Daikon radish (also called mooli): a long, white Japanese radish.
Dark sesame oil (also called Oriental sesame oil): a dark seasoning oil, high in polyunsaturated fats, made from toasted sesame seeds. Because the oil has a relatively low smoking point, it is rarely heated. Dark sesame oil should not be confused or replaced with lighter sesame cooking oils.
Debeard: to remove the fibrous threads from a mussel. These tough threads, called the beard, are produced by the mussel to attach itself to stationary objects. See also Mussel.
Devein: to remove the intestinal vein located along the outer curve of a prawn. Generally done for the sake of appearance. It is easier to remove the vein before cooking the prawn. To do so, first peel the prawn; then make a small cut along the line of the vein. Remove the vein manually or rinse the prawn under cold running water. See also Prawn.
Dijon mustard: a smooth or grainy hot mustard once manufactured only in Dijon, France; may be flavoured with herbs, green peppercorns or white wine.
Dolphin fish: see Mahimahi.
Dover sole: a lean highly prized flat fish native to the waters around Great Britain, with firm white flesh and a delicate flavour.
Dressed: refers to a fish that has had its scales, viscera, head, gills and tail removed, and often its fins as well.
Dublin Bay prawn (also called Norway lobster, scampi or langoustine): a large crustacean found in the Atlantic, Mediterranean and Adriatic. The meat, mainly in the tail, is firm and sweet.
Eel: an Atlantic fish that resembles a snake, with firm, rich flesh and a mild flavour. Eels migrate down-river to the sea to spawn. They are generally skinned before they are cooked.
Endive: a green leafy vegetable with slightly bitter-tasting leaves, often used in salads.
Fennel: a herb (also called wild fennel) whose feathery leaves and dried seeds have a mild anise flavour and are much used for flavouring. Its vegetable relative, the bulb — or Florence — fennel (also called finocchio), can be either cooked, or eaten raw in salads.
Fermented black beans: soya beans that have been fermented, dried and salted; used in Chinese dishes. The beans are often rinsed and crushed before use.
Fillet: a full-length section of a fish cut from the ribs and backbone. Also the act of removing a fillet from a fish (pages 130-131).
Flat fish: flat-bodied fish that swim horizontally along the sea bottom and have both eyes on the same side of the head. Flat fish are easy to fillet and generally are quite lean. See also Flounder; Halibut; Plaice; Sole; Turbot.
Flounder: a flat fish found in the Atlantic from the Mediterranean to the White Sea, and in the Baltic Sea. Flounder is an important food fish in northern Europe.
Freshwater bream: a carp-like fish found in lakes and rivers throughout most of Europe.
Ginger: the spicy, buff-coloured root of the ginger plant, used as a seasoning either in fresh form or dried and powdered. The dried form is not a good substitute for the fresh.
Gratin: a baked dish with a crunchy topping of breadcrumbs or grated cheese that has been browned in the oven or under the grill.
Grayling: a freshwater fish of the salmon family. Grayling is white-fleshed and firm like trout.
Grey mullet: see Mullet, grey.
Grouper: a fish caught in temperate and tropical waters around the world. Its flesh is lean, moist and sweet. Depending on the species, groupers range in

size from 500 g to 320 kg (1 to 700 lb).
Haddock: a silvery-grey member of the cod family, with lean, delicately flavoured flesh. The average weight of haddock is 1 to 2.5 kg (2 to 5 lb); it is caught in the Atlantic.
Hake: a small member of the cod family, found in the Atlantic, that weighs 500 g to 1 kg (1 to 2 lb) on average. Hake's lean, mild-flavoured flesh is somewhat softer than that of cod.
Halibut: the largest of the flat fish, with lean, moist, firm, white flesh. Fished in both the Atlantic and Pacific Oceans, halibut can weigh as much as 320 kg (700 lb). Because of its large size, halibut is generally cut up and marketed in steak or fillet form.
Hazelnut: the nut of the hazel shrub or tree. It is rich in oil, with a mild, smoky taste. Hazelnuts are eaten raw or used in sweet cooked dishes.
Herring: a small fish, weighing from 250 to 750 g (½ to 1½ lb), dwelling in large schools in the Atlantic and Pacific Oceans and the North Sea. The flesh is off-white, rich and soft. Cured herrings are available in many different forms — kippers, bloaters and rollmops are just three examples.
Jerusalem artichoke: neither an artichoke nor from Jerusalem, this vegetable is the tuberous root of a member of the sunflower family. In texture, colour and flavour, it resembles the water chestnut. "Jerusalem" may derive from the Italian word "girasole", meaning a plant whose flowers turn towards the sun.
John Dory: a plump, flattish fish with an ugly face, the John Dory is found in the Atlantic and Mediterranean. The flesh is white and delicate like sole and turbot.
Julienne: the French term for vegetables or other food cut into strips.
Lemon sole: not a true sole, this flat fish is an important food fish in Britain and France.
Littleneck clam: sometimes called quahog, this small hard-shell clam is a native of the east coast of the United States. It is also found in Britain, France and Ireland. It should not be confused with the Pacific littleneck clam, which is a soft-shelled mollusc.
Lobster: a crustacean with a long body and five pairs of jointed legs, the first of which have pincers. The European or common lobster is found in the Atlantic from the far north down to the Bay of Biscay. See also Spiny lobster.
Mace: the ground aril, or covering, that encases the nutmeg seed.
Mackerel: a rich-fleshed fish, weighing 500 g to 2 kg (1 to 4 lb). Mackerel's firm flesh, high in oil, flakes easily and lightens in colour when cooked.
Madeira: a fortified wine, often used in cooking, that is produced on the island of Madeira. There are four classes of Madeira, ranging from sweet to dry in flavour and brown to gold in colour.
Mahimahi: the Hawaiian name for dolphin fish, which is caught in semitropical waters of the Pacific and Atlantic Oceans as well as in the Mediterranean. Its size varies from 1 to 22 kg (2 to 50 lb); the flesh is lean, firm and flavourful.
Mange-tout: small, flat green pea pods, eaten whole with only the stems and strings removed.
Mantle: another name for the body pouch of the squid. It can be sliced or left whole and stuffed.
Marjoram: sweet marjoram and its heartier relative pot marjoram are aromatic herbs related to oregano, but milder in flavour.
Marsala: a fortified dessert wine named after the region of Sicily where it originated. Most varieties are sweet in flavour and and brown in colour.
Mirin: a sweetened Japanese cooking wine made from rice. If mirin is unavailable, substitute white wine or sake mixed with an equal amount of sugar.
Monkfish (also called angler-fish): an Atlantic fish with a scaleless, thick-skinned body and an enormous, ugly head; only the tail portion, however, is edible. Although the monkfish weighs on average 3.5 to 7.5 kg (8 to 15 lb), some specimens grow as large as 22 kg (50 lb). The lean, firm, somewhat dry flesh is thought by some to resemble lobster in flavour.
Monounsaturated fats: one of the three types of fats found in foods. Monounsaturated fats are believed not to raise the level of cholesterol in the blood.
Mullet, grey: this attractive, silvery blue-grey fish is found in the Atlantic and Mediterranean. The firm yet delicate flesh is somewhat like mackerel although less rich. In the eastern Mediterranean, the roe is used to make *taramasalata*.
Mullet, red: a delicious fish, the red mullet is small, weighing between 175 and 500 g (6 oz and 1 lb). The liver is greatly prized.
Mushrooms, dried Asian: before use, dried Asian mushrooms must be covered with boiling water and soaked for at least 20 minutes, then trimmed of their woody stems. To use the mushroom-soaking liquid as a flavouring agent, pour off and reserve the clear liquid; discard any sand that settles to the bottom. Soaked mushrooms can be stored in plastic film in the refrigerator. See also Shiitake mushroom.
Mussel: a bivalve mollusc with bluish-black shells found along Atlantic and Pacific coasts as well as in the Mediterranean. The mussel's sweet flesh varies from beige to orange-yellow in colour when cooked. See also Debeard; Purge.
Non-reactive pan: a cooking vessel whose surface does not chemically react with food. Materials used include stainless steel, enamel, glass and some alloys. Untreated cast iron and aluminium may react with acids, producing discoloration or a peculiar taste.
Nori: paper-like dark green or black sheets of dried seaweed that are often used in Japanese cooking as flavouring or as wrappers for rice and vegetables.
Norway haddock: a plump fish, usually sold in fillets, that is found in the cold northerly waters of the Atlantic Ocean. The Norway haddock is closely related to the redfish.
Octopus: a shell-less mollusc of the cephalopod family that inhabits the Atlantic and Pacific as well as the Mediterranean. Octopuses have soft bodies that include an ink sac and attached to it, eight tentacles covered with suction cups. The usual market size of an octopus is 1.25 kg (2½ lb) or less, and most are sold cleaned. The meat is white and mild flavoured and is sometimes served in the ink.
Olive oil: any of various grades of cooking oil extracted from olives. Extra virgin oil has a full, fruity flavour and the lowest acidity. Virgin olive oil is slightly higher in acidity and lighter in flavour. Pure olive oil, a processed blend of olive oils, has the highest acidity and the lightest taste.
Orzo: a rice-shaped dried pasta made of semolina. The word means "barley" in Italian.
Oyster: a bivalve mollusc with two dissimilar shells, found on the Atlantic coasts down to the Mediterranean, in the shallow waters of bays and estuaries. The size, shape and taste of oysters are determined by the waters in which they grow and the time of year they are harvested. When water temperatures rise, the oysters become more watery in texture, which leads some to say that oysters taste best in cold winter months. France is the biggest producer of oysters in Europe, and its high-quality oysters such as *fines de claire* are justly famous. Excellent oysters are also farmed in Britain, Belgium, the Netherlands and Denmark.
Papaya (also called pawpaw): a fruit native to Central America. The colour of the skin ranges from green to orange, and the flesh from pale yellow to salmon. When ripe, the fruit is sweet and enjoyed raw, but unripe papayas may be eaten cooked as a vegetable.
Paprika: a slightly sweet, bright-red powder produced by grinding dried sweet red peppers. The best paprika is Hungarian.
Pectoral fins: a pair of fins located behind the gills of a fish.
Pen (also called quill): a piece of cartilage located in the body pouch, or mantle, of a squid. The pen serves as the squid's support structure and should be removed before the squid is cooked. See also Squid.
Perch: a spiny-finned freshwater fish, weighing from 500 g to 9 kg (1 to 20 lb), the perch is somewhat bony but much prized for the flavour of its firm, fine-grained flesh. It should be scaled as soon as possible after it is caught; alternatively, blanching it before scaling makes the job easier.
Phyllo (or filo): a paper-thin flour-and-water pastry popular in Greece and the Middle East. It can be made at home or bought, fresh or frozen, from delicatessens and shops specializing in Middle-Eastern food.
Pike: a freshwater fish commercially available in late spring and summer. The flesh is lean, white and easily flaked when cooked.
Plaice: a flat fish abundant in the European Atlantic, plaice is considered to be inferior to sole and turbot.
Plaki: a Greek fish dish baked on a bed of tomatoes.
Poach: to cook gently in simmering liquid. The temperature of the poaching liquid should be approximately 94°C (200°F), and its surface should merely tremble. Fish is poached in wine, stock or court-bouillon. This cooking method keeps food moist and adds flavour to it.
Polyunsaturated fats: one of the three types of fats found in foods. They exist in abundance in such vegetable oils as safflower, sunflower, corn and soya bean. They are also found in seafood. Certain highly polyunsaturated fatty acids called omega-3s occur exclusively in seafood and marine animals. Polyunsaturated fats lower the level of cholesterol in the blood.
Powan: also called whitefish and vendace, this fish is caught in freshwater lakes and rivers in Great Britain and Europe.
Prawn: a crustacean that lives in cold and warm waters in all parts of the world, called prawn or shrimp (or both) depending on local preference and size. There are hundreds of species, from the huge Asian striped tiger prawn and large Mediterranean prawn, to the medium-sized deep-water prawn of the North Atlantic and the tiny brown shrimp. Prawns and shrimps can be cooked in or out of the shell. They are moderately high in cholesterol but very low in fat. See also Devein and Dublin Bay prawn.
Prosciutto: an uncooked, dry-cured and slightly salty Italian ham, sliced paper-thin.
Provolone: a hard, plastic-curd Italian cheese, creamy white with a golden-yellow rind and available in a variety of shapes and sizes. *Dolce provolone* is not aged and has a fairly mild flavour; *piccante provolone* is aged for a more pronounced flavour.
Purée: to reduce food to a smooth, even, pulp-like consistency by mashing it, passing it through a sieve, or processing it in a blender or food processor.
Puréed tomatoes: purée made from skinned fresh or canned tomatoes. Available commercially, but should not be confused with the thicker, concentrated tomato paste which is sometimes labelled tomato purée.
Purge: to cleanse bivalve molluscs of sand and grit. Not absolutely necessary, but done to clams and mussels (page 103).
Quill: see Pen.
Radicchio: a red chicory of Italian origin with a

refreshingly bitter taste, radicchio is frequently used in salads.
Ramekin: a small, round, straight-sided glass or porcelain mould, used to bake a single serving of food.
Recommended Daily Amount (RDA): the average daily amount of an essential nutrient recommended for healthy people by the U.K. Department of Health and Social Security.
Red mullet: see Mullet, red.
Red snapper: a bright red Atlantic fish weighing between 1 and 3 kg (2 and 6 lb) with red eyes.
Redfish: see Norway haddock.
Reduce: to boil down a liquid in order to concentrate its flavour or thicken its consistency.
Refresh: to rinse a cooked vegetable under cold running water to arrest its cooking and set its colour.
Rice vinegar: a mild, fragrant vinegar that is less assertive than cider vinegar or distilled white vinegar. It is available in dark, light, seasoned and sweetened varieties. Japanese rice vinegar generally is milder than the Chinese variety.
Rice wine: Chinese rice wine (shao-hsing) is brewed from rice and wine. Japanese rice wine (sake) has a different flavour but may be used as a substitute. If rice wine is not available, use sherry in its place. See also Mirin.
Roe: refers primarily to fish eggs, but edible roe is also found in scallops, crabs and lobsters.
Safflower oil: a vegetable oil that contains the highest proportion of polyunsaturated fats of all the vegetable oils generally available.
Saffron: the dried, yellowish-red stigmas (or threads) of the flower of *Crocus sativus*; saffron yields a pungent flavour and a brilliant yellow colour. Although powdered saffron may be substituted for the threads, it has less flavour.
Salmon: a sea fish, the salmon migrates to freshwater rivers and lakes to spawn. It can weigh 3 to 13 kg (7 to 30 lb). Much of the commercial supply is farm-raised and is often sold cut into steaks and cutlets. Baltic salmon has paler pink flesh than Atlantic salmon, and a higher fat content.
Sardine: an immature pilchard, the sardine is fished in the warmer waters of the Atlantic and in the Mediterranean. Because it is a relatively fatty fish, fresh (or frozen) sardines are delicious simply gutted and grilled.
Saturated fats: one of the three types of fats found in foods. They exist in abundance in animal products and coconut and palm oils; they raise the levels of cholesterol in the blood. Because high blood-cholesterol levels may cause heart disease, saturated fat consumption should be restricted to less than 15 per cent of the calories provided by the daily diet.
Sauté: to cook food quickly in a small amount of butter or oil over high heat, stirring or tossing the food often to keep it from burning or sticking.
Scale: to remove the small, plate-like structures covering most fish.
Scallop: a bivalve mollusc found throughout the world, in the Atlantic from Iceland to Spain and in the Pacific from Alaska to Australia. The white nut of meat (actually the adductor muscle) and the orange roe, or coral, are eaten. Tiny queen scallops are a different species from the familiar larger scallops known in France as *coquilles Saint-Jacques*.
Sea bass: a handsome fish with firm, lean flesh, the sea bass is found in the Atlantic. In the summer, sea bass are also caught by anglers in coastal waters.
Sea bream: a number of fish that are found in the warmer waters of the Mediterranean and Atlantic. Only one species, the red sea bream, is common in European Atlantic waters. Sea bream are usually small — 750 g to 1 kg (1½ to 2 lb) — and sold whole.
Sea trout: see Trout, sea.
Sesame oil: see Dark sesame oil.
Seviche (or ceviche): originally a Peruvian dish made of raw fish or scallops combined with lemon or lime juice, onion, crushed red pepper flakes and black peppercorns. The term is now used to describe any dish in which fish or shellfish is marinated in citrus juice. The acid in the juice breaks down the protein, thus "cooking" the raw fish or shellfish.
Shad: a bony Atlantic fish that is a member of the herring family. Shad swim up-river to spawn; the roe is highly prized.
Shallot: a mild variety of the onion, with a subtle flavour and papery, red-brown skin.
Shark: a primitive fish without bones or scales found in both the Atlantic and the Pacific Oceans. The flesh, similar to that of swordfish, is lean yet full-flavoured, firm and dense. Dogfish, also called huss, flake or rigg, is a member of the shark family.
Shiitake mushroom: a strongly flavoured mushroom originally cultivated in Japan. It is sold fresh or dried; the dried version should be stored in a cool, dry place and may be reconstituted by soaking in warm water.
Shoyu: see Soy sauce.
Shrimp: see Prawn.
Shuck: to remove the meat from the shells of a bivalve mollusc.
Simmer: to cook a liquid or sauce just below its boiling point so that the liquid's surface barely ripples.
Skate: a flat, scaleless, diamond-shaped fish with enlarged pectoral fins called wings; skate is found both in the Atlantic and in the Pacific. The myriad varieties of skate range in weight from 1 to 50 kg (2 to 100 lb). The wings provide delicious meat, whose texture and taste — firm and quite sweet — resemble those of scallops.
Sodium: a nutrient essential to maintaining the proper balance of fluids in the body. In most diets, a major source of the element is table salt, made up of 40 per cent sodium. Excess sodium may contribute to high blood pressure, which increases the risk of heart disease. One teaspoon (5.5 g) of salt, with 2,132 milligrams of sodium, contains just over the maximum daily amount that is recommended by the World Health Organization.
Sole: see Dover sole; Lemon sole.
Soy sauce: a savoury, salty, brown liquid made from fermented soya beans. One tablespoon of ordinary soy sauce contains 1,030 milligrams of sodium; lower-sodium variations, such as the naturally fermented shoyu, used in the recipes in this book, may contain as little as half that amount.
Spiny lobster (also called rock lobster, crawfish or langouste): although called a lobster, this crustacean lacks the huge claws of the true lobster. The spiny lobster is rarely found further north than south-west England and the supply in Europe is limited.
Squid: a shell-less mollusc of the cephalopod family found in the Atlantic and Mediterranean. The two main varieties are short-finned and long-finned squid. Eighty per cent of the squid — including the tentacles, body pouch, fins and ink — is edible. If it is bought whole, the pen, beak, ink sac and gonads should be removed before the squid is consumed. Squid is high in cholesterol. See also Mantle; Pen.
Steam: to cook food in the vapour from boiling water; steaming is one of the best cooking techniques for preserving nutrients and flavours.
Stir-fry: to cook small, uniformly cut vegetables, fish or meat over high heat in a small amount of oil, stirring constantly to ensure even cooking in a short time. The traditional cooking vessel is a Chinese wok; a heavy-bottomed frying pan may also be used.
Stock: a savoury liquid made by simmering aromatic vegetables, herbs and spices — and meat or poultry bones and trimmings — in water. A vegetarian stock can also be made. Stock forms a flavour-rich base for sauces.
Sun-dried tomatoes: Italian plum tomatoes that are air-dried to concentrate their flavour, and often packed in oil.
Sweet chili sauce: any of a group of Asian sauces containing chilies, vinegar, sugar and salt. Such a sauce may be used as a condiment to accompany fish, meat or poultry, or it may be included as an ingredient in a dish.
Swordfish: a large fish, weighing between 90 and 225 kg (200 and 500 lb), found throughout the world from the Atlantic and Pacific Oceans to the Mediterranean. Usually sold in steak form, the flesh is lean, dense and creamy white to pink in colour, except for small dark patches.
Tabasco sauce: a hot, unsweetened chili sauce. A similar Asian version is the Thai sriracha sauce.
Tarragon: a strong herb with a sweet anise taste. In combination with other herbs — notably sage, rosemary and thyme — it should be used sparingly to avoid a clash of flavours. Because heat intensifies the herb's flavour, cooked dishes require smaller amounts of tarragon.
Thyme: a versatile herb with a zesty, slightly fruity flavour, and strong aroma.
Timbale: a creamy mixture of vegetables, meat or fish baked in a mould. The term, which is French for "kettledrum", also denotes a drum-shaped baking dish.
Tomalley: the greenish liver of a lobster that is savoured by itself or used as a flavouring agent.
Tomatillo (also called Mexican ground cherry): a small, tart, green tomato-like fruit used as a vegetable, particularly in Mexican dishes. It is covered with a loose, papery husk and is closely related to the sweeter Cape gooseberry.
Tomato paste: a concentrated tomato purée, available in cans and tubes, used in sauces and soups. See also Puréed tomatoes.
Total fat: an individual's daily intake of polyunsaturated, monounsaturated and saturated fats. Nutritionists recommend that fats provide no more than 35 per cent of the energy in the diet. The term as used in this book refers to the combined fats in a given dish or food.
Trout: a freshwater fish with firm, fatty flesh; weight can vary considerably, but the usual size is 1 to 4.5 kg (2 to 10 lb).
Trout, rainbow: a freshwater fish, with an average weight of 250 to 500 g (½ to 1 lb). Most of the commercial supply is farm-raised. The flesh is soft and rich in flavour.
Trout, sea (also called salmon trout): of the same species as the brown river trout, the sea trout has a migratory life and habits similar to salmon, which is why it is also called salmon trout. The flesh is pale pink and moist with an excellent flavour and texture.
Tuna: refers to several varieties of fish, found in both the Atlantic and the Pacific; some tuna can weigh as much as 675 kg (1,500 lb). The flesh is dense, full-flavoured and oily; it can be white, as in long-finned or albacore tuna, or light brown, as in bigeye and skipjack tuna. Bluefin tuna has dark, nearly red flesh.
Turbot: a flat fish whose high body-fat content (about 10 per cent) is unusual for a flat fish. Mainly fished in the North Sea, turbot is also found in the Atlantic from Iceland and Norway down to the Mediterranean. Small turbot, weighing 750 g to 1 kg (1½ to 2 lb), are called chicken turbot.
Turmeric: a yellow spice from a plant related to ginger, used as a colouring agent and occasionally as

a substitute for saffron. Turmeric has a musty odour and a slightly bitter flavour.
Virgin olive oil: see Olive oil.
Wasabi: a Japanese horseradish, usually sold in powdered form. The powder is mixed with water to form a fiery green paste, which is then served with sushi or noodles.
Water chestnut: the walnut-sized tuber of an aquatic Asian plant, with rough brown skin and white, sweet, crisp flesh. Fresh water chestnuts may be refrigerated for up to two weeks; they must be peeled before use.
White pepper: a powder ground from the same berry as that used to produce black pepper but with the berry's outer shell removed before grinding, resulting in a milder flavour. White pepper is used as a less visible alternative to black pepper in light-coloured foods.
Whiting: a member of the cod family, whiting is caught in the North Sea and the Atlantic. The flesh is delicate and sweet.
Wild rice: the seed of a water grass native to the Great Lakes region of the United States. It is appreciated for its nutty flavour and chewy texture.
Yogurt: a smooth-textured, semi-solid cultured milk product made with varying percentages of fat. Yogurt makes an excellent substitute for soured cream in cooking. Yogurt may also be combined with soured cream to produce a sauce or topping that is lower in fat and calories than soured cream alone.

Index

Picture Credits

All of the photographs in *Fresh Ways with Fish and Shellfish* were taken by staff photographer Renée Comet unless otherwise indicated:
Cover: James Murphy. 2: top and centre, Carolyn Wall Rothery. 4: right centre, John Elliott. 5: lower left, Michael Latil; upper right and lower right, John Elliott. 6: John D. Dawson. 14-17: John Elliott. 19: John Elliott. 27: John Elliott. 31: above, Michael Latil. 35: Steven Biver. 36: John Elliott. 39: Aldo Tutino. 42: John Elliott. 44: Aldo Tutino. 46: Steven Biver. 52: John Elliott. 53: Michael Latil. 54: John Elliott. 56: Steven Biver. 57: John Elliott. 59: John Elliott. 60: below, Michael Latil. 62-63: John Elliott. 66: Michael Latil. 75: John Elliott. 77: John Elliott. 79-80: John Elliott. 84: John Elliott. 87: Michael Latil. 89: Michael Latil. 90-91: Michael Latil. 97-100: Michael Latil. 102: Michael Latil. 104-107: Michael Latil. 109-110: Michael Latil. 119: John Elliott. 120: Michael Latil. 123: John Elliott. 124-126: Michael Latil. 128-131: John Elliott. 132: Taran Z. 133: John Elliott. 134: above, John Elliott; below, Taran Z. 135: Taran Z.

Acknowledgements

The editors are particularly indebted to the following people: Mary Jane Blandford, Alexandria, Va., U.S.A.; Nora Carey, Versailles, France; Robert Carmack, Camas, Wash., U.S.A.; Sharon Farrington, Bethesda, Md., U.S.A.; Carol Gvozdich, Alexandria, Va., U.S.A.; Maggie Heinz, London; Nancy Lendved, Alexandria, Va., U.S.A.; Faye Levy, Santa Monica, Calif., U.S.A.; Tajvana Queen, Alexandria, Va., U.S.A.; Ann Ready, Alexandria, Va., U.S.A.; Rita Walters, London; CiCi Williamson, Alexandria, Va., U.S.A.; Sarah Wiley, London.

The editors also wish to thank: Alaska Fisheries Development Foundation, Anchorage, Alaska; Alaska Seafood Marketing Institute, Juneau, Alaska; The Amber Grain, Washington, D.C.; Moira Banks, London; Jim Barklow, Jake's Famous Crawfish and Seafoods, Inc., Portland, Ore., U.S.A.; Martha Blacksall, BBH Corporation, Washington, D.C.; Jo Calabrese, Royal Worcester Spode Inc., New York, N.Y.; Jackie Chalkley, Washington, D.C.; Chicago Fish House, Chicago, Ill., U.S.A.; Nic Colling, Home Produce Company, Alexandria, Va., U.S.A.; Gene Cope, Lou Kissel, National Marine Fisheries Service, Department of Commerce, Washington, D.C.; Jeanne Dale, The Pilgrim Glass Corp., New York, N.Y.; Paul Dexter, Salvatore Termini, Deruta of Italy Corp., New York, N.Y.; Rex Downey, Oxon Hill, Md., U.S.A.; Dr. Jacob Exler, U.S. Department of Agriculture, Hyattsville, Md., U.S.A.; Nancy Fennel, Oregon Dungeness Crab Commission, Salem, Ore., U.S.A.; Dr. George Flick, Virginia Polytechnic Institute, Blacksburg, Va., U.S.A.; Flowers Unique, Inc., Alexandria, Va., U.S.A.; Food Marketing Institute, Washington, D.C.; Giant Food, Inc., Landover, Md., U.S.A.; E. Goodwin & Sons, Inc., Jessup, Md., U.S.A.; Great Lakes Fisheries Development Foundation, Grand Haven, Mich., U.S.A.; Gulf and South Atlantic Fisheries Development Foundation, Tampa, Fla., U.S.A.; Chong Su Han, Grass Roots Restaurant, Alexandria, Va., U.S.A.; Wretha Hanson, Franz Bader Gallery, Washington, D.C.; Kathy Hardesty, Columbia, Md., U.S.A.; Steven Himmelfarb, U.S. Fish, Inc., Kensington, Md., U.S.A.; Robert Jordan, Jordan Seafood, Inc., Washington, D.C.; Gary Latzman, Kirk Phillips, Retroneu, New York, N.Y.; Richard Lord, Fulton Market Information Service, New York, N.Y.; Metropolitan Ice and Storage, Washington, D.C.; Mid-Atlantic Fisheries Development Foundation, Inc., Annapolis, Md., U.S.A.; Jorge Mora, Mora Camera Services, Washington, D.C.; Mutual Fish Company, Inc., Seattle, Wash., U.S.A.; Ed Nash, The American Hand Plus, Washington, D.C.; New England Fisheries Development Foundation, Boston, Mass., U.S.A.; Lisa Ownby, Alexandria, Va., U.S.A.; Joyce Piotrowski, Vienna, Va., U.S.A.; Pruitt Seafood, Washington, D.C.; Linda Robertson, JUD Tile, Vienna, Va., U.S.A.; Jon Rowley, Fishworks, Seattle, Wash.; Safeway Stores, Inc., Landover, Md., U.S.A.; Bert Saunders, WILTON Armetale, New York, N.Y.; James Simmons, Washington Fish Exchange, Inc., Alexandria, Va., U.S.A.; Greg Smith, Nikon Professional Services, Washington, D.C.; Straight from the Crate, Inc., Alexandria, Va., U.S.A.; Sutton Place Gourmet, Washington, D.C.; Triple M Seafood, Pompano Beach, Fla., U.S.A.; West Coast Fisheries Development Foundation, Portland, Ore., U.S.A.; Williams-Sonoma, Washington, D.C.; Tere Yow, Vietri, Inc., Chapel Hill, N.C., U.S.A.

Props for the European edition: 14: platter, Villeroy & Boch, Harrods, London; 16: plate, Harrods, London; 19: terracotta plate, Elizabeth David Ltd., London; 36: Fleuron platter and sauceboat, Harrods, London; 54: baking dish, Elizabeth David Ltd., London; 62: oval baking dish, Elizabeth David Ltd., London; 77: platter, Reject China Shop, London; sauceboat and oval plate, Elizabeth David Ltd., London; 80: platter, Reject China Shop, London.

Typesetting by G. Beard and Son Ltd., Brighton, Sussex, England
Printed and bound by Brepols S.A., Turnhout, Belgium